RENAISSANCE DRAMA AND A MODERN AUDIENCE

By the same author

JOHN MARSTON'S PLAYS: Theme, Structure and Performance

RENAISSANCE DRAMA AND A MODERN AUDIENCE

Michael Scott

M

© Michael Scott 1982

All rights reserved. No part of this publication may be reproduced or transmitted, in any form or by any means, without permission

First published 1982 by
THE MACMILLAN PRESS LTD
*London and Basingstoke
Companies and representatives
throughout the world*

ISBN 0 333 27599 3

*Phototypeset in Great Britain by
Tradespools Ltd, Frome, Somerset
Printed in Hong Kong*

To my parents

Contents

Acknowledgements ix

Introduction xi

1 The Comedy of Errors   1

2 Dr Faustus   18

3 The Revenger's Tragedy   31

4 Volpone   47

5 Measure for Measure   61

6 The Changeling   76

7 'Tis Pity She's a Whore   89

8 Postscript   105

Abbreviations   108

Notes and References   109

Index   124

Acknowledgements

I am grateful to Trevor Nunn, Joint Artistic Director, and John Barton, Associate Director of the Royal Shakespeare Company, for permission to reprint material from prompt-books and programmes of recent RSC productions; to Dr Anne Barton for permission to quote from her article in the RSC programme for the 1970 production of *Measure for Measure*; to Brian Shelton and the Pitlochry Festival Theatre for permission to employ material from Mr Shelton's rehearsal notes for his 1965 production of *The Revenger's Tragedy*.

Introduction

The purpose of this book is to introduce those interested in reading, studying and watching late-sixteenth and early-seventeenth-century drama to the modernity inherent in seven seminal plays. Renaissance drama[1] belongs both to literature and to theatre and thus each chapter attempts to provide a critical evaluation of the given play's theme and structure and an account of some of its most recent productions on the modern British stage. In the case of *Measure for Measure* both aspects are fused into a discussion of the rich variety of the play's productions during the 1970s whilst in that of *Volpone*, for example, theatrical experience introduces an evaluation of the play's thematic appropriateness to the twentieth-century.

The plays discussed range from *The Comedy of Errors* at the beginning of the major period of Elizabethan-Jacobean writing to *'Tis Pity She's a Whore* which sees its close nearly forty years later. Despite the gaps in time and genre, common themes between these and the other five plays discussed, are stressed. Egeon and Antipholus of Syracuse like Faustus, De Flores or Giovanni are searching to find themselves. The problem of existence determines their actions whether those be humorous, tragic or sadistic. With Volpone and Angelo manipulation of others for one's own desire and aggrandisement dominates the structure of their respective plays, whilst for Vindice revenge becomes a determinant of existence in a sterile world of self-imposed decadence.

Such dramatic themes are not unfamiliar today. Common features of twentieth-century life and dramatic expression – corruption, stagnation, exploitation – form the kernel also of many renaissance plays. In text and production we find an affinity with Elizabethan protagonists and form an understanding of their problems despite our advances in science or philosophy. If we did not the plays would have perished long ago. Audience susceptibilities however change from age to age as the balance veers from optimism to pessimism and back again. Consequently there are areas of the works and indeed some entire plays, that speak to us more acutely than they did, for example, to eighteenth- or nineteenth-century readers or audiences and similarly there are aspects which no longer seem to hold the force they once did. The nature of drama is such that it is recreated for the age that produces and witnesses it and thus the intention here is to point to those areas in the plays which the late twentieth century seems to find most arresting.

My thanks are due to many people who have helped to make this book possible. Dr Gordon Williams of the University of Wales in reading through the work in progress has made many helpful suggestions which have been incorporated into the text. Jeremy Hawthorn and Emrys Hughes at Sunderland Polytechnic have provided every encouragement throughout the venture, whilst my wife, as ever, has shared the work, helped in the production research, read through the draft copies and discussed its progress and content from the beginning. My gratitude is expressed to Miss T. M. O'Reilly, who produced the typescript, and to the staff of the following libraries and theatres who have been generous with their time and help: Durham University Library; Sunderland Polytechnic Library; the British Library; the Shakespeare Centre Library; the Theatre Museum; the Royal Shakespeare Theatre; the National Theatre; the Pitlochry Festival Theatre; Nottingham Playhouse. To all those who have helped in other ways, family, friends and colleagues, my thanks.

M. S.

1 The Comedy of Errors

The Comedy of Errors is a farce and as such belongs to an art form relying for its strength and theme on the ingenuity of its structure. From Plautus to Ayckbourn farce has exploited social archetypes and institutions so as to entertain its audiences by laughing at the world and its absurdities. The process is naturally thematic, the social, moral or psychological content being an integral part of its dramatic form and balance.[1] Thus the aesthetic success of good farce depends on its structure and it is from this viewpoint that any criticism must begin its evaluation. So it has been in recent years with *The Comedy of Errors* where scholars have focused upon two principal issues, the introduction in the final scene of the Abbess as a structural device to reconcile the 'errors' of the plot, and the sentence of death passed on Egeon at the beginning of the play and foreshadowing all the festivities.

To the fore of those criticizing the 'clumsy' introduction of Emilia has been Bertrand Evans:

> When we learn that there is an Abbess in Ephesus and that this Abbess is no other than old Aegeon's lost wife, the play is within eighty lines of the end. Had we been told of her existence at the outset, we would have been assured, even while recollection of Aegeon's desperate plight shadowed the hilarious scenes, that all would finally be well. As the play stands, with only half of the frame – Aegeon's plight – presented to us at the outset, it is plain that the dramatist has simply deceived us. He makes us believe our view complete when it is only partial ... By introducing Aemilia early in the action, Shakespeare could have added another level to the structure of awareness and thus have increased the complexity of our responses.[2]

Although arresting, such criticism is not altogether correct, since through allowing the audience to realize Emilia's role of reconciliation too early in the work Shakespeare might well have over-simplified his play and thus reduced rather than increased the complexity of response. Further such action would have naturally upset the structural-thematic balance of the play which, as will be shown, largely depends on the audience being unaware of Emilia's healing presence until the final act. Professor Evans however does point us in an interesting direction since he correctly implies that there is some form of correspondence between Egeon's 'desperate plight' and Emilia's therapeutic role.

This becomes more evident when the second structural issue of the work is examined, that of Egeon's sentence of death in the first scene. Leo Salingar has admirably illustrated the precise tone set by this serious opening to the play. It is not one of tragedy but of romance:

> The experienced playgoer at an early performance would not have been misled ... He could hardly have anticipated the fast and funny movement of the rest of the play, but he could have recognised in the opening scene the distinctive notes of romance rather than tragedy; in the speaker's inclination towards pathos rather than aggressiveness, for example, and in Egeon's reference to Fortune, which had left him something 'to delight in' as well as something 'to sorrow for'.[3]

Salingar continues by showing the work's relationship to established romance conventions thus enabling him to assert 'that from the outset, both forms of the story of family reunion, the romantic and the farcical, were present to [Shakespeare's] mind together' (p. 67). It is this fusion of the romance and the farce which helps the play build on its Plautine and romance models in establishing a thematic structure around the marriage convention.

Egeon in the first scene is a pathetic old man, isolated in an alien land divorced from wife and children through the dictates of wealth and Fortune:

> In Syracusa was I born, and wed
> Unto a woman happy but for me,

> And by me, – had not our hap been bad.
> With her I liv'd in joy; our wealth increas'd
> By prosperous voyages I often made
> To Epidamnum, till my factor's death,
> And the great care of goods at random left,
> Drew me from the kind embracements of my spouse.
> (I. i. 36–43)[4]

This incident was eventually to isolate Egeon from wife and children so that now in Ephesus he has no will to live, his only wish being to know whether his family are still alive:

> ... here must end the story of my life,
> And happy were I in my timely death,
> Could all my travels warrant me they live.
>
> Hopeless and helpless doth Egeon wend,
> But to procrastinate his lifeless end. (I. i. 137–9, 157–8)

The 'procrastination' of his death implies that Egeon has spent the last five years, at least, of his life in the despair of isolation, searching for his family, his roots which are his identity. It is this loss of self-identity not only for Egeon but for all his relations which is to form the kernel of the play; a simple idea at first only proposed by the old man's pathetic tale but soon stated explicitly as a theme, by Antipholus of Syracuse:

> He that commends me to mine own content
> Commends me to the thing I cannot get.
> I to the world am like a drop of water
> That in the ocean seeks another drop,
> Who, falling there to find his fellow forth,
> (Unseen, inquisitive) confounds himself.
> So I, to find a mother and a brother,
> In quest of them, unhappy, lose myself. (I. ii. 33–40)

It is misleading to see this statement as an insight to Antipholus's characterization. We are not watching a comedy dealing in such terms but rather a farce which negates characterization in favour of simple archetype. Antipholus's speech therefore naturally becomes a clarification of Egeon's opening statement. In this respect the play operates very similarly to a musical score which may begin with an orchestral embellishment before the theme is simply stated by a single instrument, to be then followed by an intricate set of variations.[5] Thus Egeon's exposition is simply clarified by Antipholus before we are presented with the complexities of the variations, which in this case we call the 'errors' on the theme of the loss of identity. We soon find therefore that the three principal characters, Antipholus of Syracuse, Antipholus of Ephesus, and Adriana are comically portrayed as separated from any relationship with another person. All are searching, striving, enquiring and yet getting nowhere since there seem to be no answers. In both philosophical and dramatic terms, in the twentieth-century, this depiction of separation and utter loneliness has found expression in the farcical theatre of the absurd, Adamov for example crying out:

> What is there? I know first of all that I am. But who am I? All I know of myself is that I suffer. And if I suffer it is because at the origin of myself there is mutilation, separation.
> I am separated. What am I separated from – I cannot name it. But I am separated.[6]

Thus the absurd theatre presents the modern audience with empty stereotype figures waiting, sleeping, collecting, eating, babbling, raging, emptily explaining, falsely reasoning. Shakespeare in this farce is not greatly concerned with what we now might see as the absurdists' metaphysical ethic[7] but his dramatic score in *The Comedy of Errors* does employ similar vacuous activities in order to illustrate the loneliness of man devoid of roots whether they be in the context of father, mother, brother or wife. The individual's separation from the family is his absurdity and it is this which finds central expression in the play's portrayal of the Antipholus of Ephesus–Adriana relationship.

To understand fully the complexity of their marriage in the context of the dramatic structure it is necessary to be aware of the correspondence between the twin brothers. Although, in line with Aristotelean principles, there is only one action in *The Comedy of Errors* there are within it two sets of adventures, those of Antipholus of Syracuse and those of Antipholus of Ephesus. For them Empson's concept of correspondence is operative, 'once you take the two parts to correspond, any character may take on *mana* because he seems to cause what he corresponds to or be Logos of what he symbolises'.[8] The fact that the Antipholuses are twins immediately signifies that we are meant to understand a correspondence between them and similarly between the two Dromios. Further because of the relationship between the Dromios and Antipholuses there is also some form of correspondence implied between all four characters born 'That very hour, and in the self-same inn' (I. i. 53). Each of the four by correspondence represents or reflects certain facets of the other's personality, aspirations and difficulties.[9] This is particularly so of the Antipholuses in relation to Adriana since as with farce throughout the ages, much of the play's humour depends on marital problems and intrigues. Quite correctly the marriage debate in the work has often been stressed by critics[10] but perhaps what has not been emphasized enough is the way in which both of the twins reflect Adriana's difficulties with her husband. The wife's first appearance sees her complaining of her lot as a woman:

Why should their liberty than ours be more? (II. i. 10)

A valid question especially for a twentieth-century audience which would no doubt find Luciana's placating replies to be repellently anachronistic. It would be wrong however to take that moral issue as the central element of their discussion, since the dramatist's main concern here is to illustrate Adriana's frustration which is derived from her love for her unresponsive husband. We are presented by her complaints with a form of negative positivism. By railing about her husband she illustrates her attachment to him. It is a common device, Shakespeare for example, employing it to great effect later in his career with his portrayals of Cleopatra and Lady Macduff. Like them therefore at the end of all the railing Adriana admits her life is totally bound up with that of her husband:

... he's master of my state.
What ruins are in me that can be found
By him not ruin'd? Then is he the ground
Of my defeatures; my decayed fair
A sunny look of his would soon repair ... (II. i. 95–9)

By the end of II.i. therefore the audience is convinced of Adriana's sincerity towards her man. Yet what the audience does not know is whether her husband is as bad as she makes out. The confrontation soon comes between the couple, Adriana making her passionate plea to him:

> How comes it now, my husband, O, how comes it,
> That thou art then estranged from thyself? –
> Thyself I call it, being strange to me,
> That undividable, incorporate,
> Am better than thy dear self's better part.
> Ah, do not tear away thyself from me;
> For know, my love, as easy mayst thou fall
> A drop of water in the breaking gulf,
> And take unmingled thence that drop again
> Without addition or diminishing,
> As take from me thyself, and not me too. (II. ii. 119–29)

Adriana here dwells on the identity of their personalities as individuals and as part of their married union. She speaks directly therefore to the essence of their very being. But he replies:

> Plead you to me fair dame? I know you not. (II. ii. 147)

In a different play such a reply would prove heart-rending as when Hal turns to Falstaff after the latter's profession of love, and disowns him;

> I know thee not, old man. Fall to thy prayers. *(Henry IV* Part Two V. iv. 47)

Antipholus's reply however causes great hilarity since unknowingly Adriana is talking not to her husband but her husband's brother. Yet it is implied, though not stressed, in the context of the play that this is exactly the reply which Adriana would have received from her husband, Antipholus of Syracuse comically corresponding to and thus in part being his twin brother. Shakespeare's farce comically distances a social problem but thereby makes it as poignant, for example, as Pinter's absurd distancing in a play such as *The Birthday Party* where Petey and Meg are shown through verbal ineptitude to be in the stagnation of the marriage:

> *Meg* Is that you, Petey? *(Pause).* Petey, is that you? *(Pause).* Petey?
> *Petey* What?
> *Meg* Is that you?
> *Petey* Yes, it's me.
> *Meg* What? *(Her face appears at the hatch.)* Are you back?
> *Petey* Yes.
> *Meg* I've got your cornflakes ready. *(She disappears and reappears.)* Here's your cornflakes. *(He rises and takes the plate from her, sits at the table, props up the paper and begins to eat.)* *(Meg enters by the kitchen door.)* Are they nice?
> *Petey* Very nice.
> *Meg* I thought they'd be nice. *(She sits at the table.)*[11]

Neither Shakespeare nor Pinter need be overtly didactic since the conversations within the context of the play's individual dramatic structure allow the thematic point to exist. With Pinter through the vacuous nature of the conversation we are able to laugh at and yet understand the corresponding nihilism of the figures' existence. Similarly with Shakespeare we laugh at the comic misunderstanding of Adriana and her unknown brother-in-law, but instinctively accept the poignancy of the true marital situation presented through the correspondence principle.

Shakespeare does not allow himself to neglect such issues once he has suggested them, and although in a farce he has no intention of over-emphasizing the serious implication of the situation he does permit himself the liberty of taking his variations on the identity-marriage theme a little further. Thus Antipholus of Syracuse decides to play along with Adriana's game, resolves that is to humour the woman as a husband might humour his wife:

> *Syr. Ant.* [*Aside.*] To me she speaks, she moves me for her theme;
> What, was I married to her in my dream?
> Or sleep I now, and think I hear all this?

What error drives our eyes and ears amiss?
Until I know this sure uncertainty,
I'll entertain the offer'd fallacy. (II. ii. 181–6)

Surprisingly the situation is not far here from Adamov and the absurdists. Antipholus in his 'dream' gropes for answers and is forced to make pretences of acceptance. Harry Levin notes that in his mouth, as in others in this play, 'The customary rhetorical questions of comedy ... become questions of existential bewilderment or expressions of comic vertigo.'[12] Striving for a self-recognition of an identity which all others seem to know:

If everyone knows us and we know none,
'Tis time to trudge, pack and be gone. (III. ii. 151–2)

Antipholus of Syracuse attempts to grasp anything which to him appears to have substance or validity. He keeps the gold chain, since at least that exists, and he attempts to woo Luciana with professions of his own identity:

Luc. Why call you me love? Call my sister so.
Syr. Ant. Thy sister's sister.
Luc. That's my sister.
Syr. Ant. No,
   It is thyself, mine own self's better part,
   Mine eye's clear eye, my dear heart's dearer heart,
   My food, my fortune, and my sweet hope's aim
   My sole earth's heaven, and my heaven's claim.
Luc. All this my sister is, or else should be.
Syr. Ant. Call thyself sister, sweet, for I am thee;
   Thee will I love, and with thee lead my life;
   Thou hast no husband yet, nor I no wife –
   Give me thy hand.
Luc. O, soft sir, hold you still;
   I'll fetch my sister to get her good will. (III. ii. 59–70)

Yet almost simultaneously he doubts the tests which he provides for himself. What is his identity? Who is he and who are they?

... 'tis high time that I were hence;
She that doth call me husband, even my soul

Doth for a wife abhor. But her fair sister,
Possess'd with such gentle sovereign grace,
Of such enchanting presence and discourse,
Hath almost made me traitor to myself;
But lest myself be guilty to self-wrong,
I'll stop mine ears against the mermaid's song. (III. ii. 156–63)

Correspondingly, Antipholus of Ephesus discovering the displacement of his identity through the prohibitions from his own house, resorts to assurances of his own masculinity and power – the crow-bar, the rope's end, the prostitute paid for by the chain. The very name of Antipholus whether he be of Ephesus or Syracuse has been usurped. Once again through a different context Shakespeare only a little later in his career was to turn such a theft into tragedy, Richard II crying out to relentless Northumberland:

No lord of thine, thou haught insulting man;
Nor no man's lord. I have no name, no title;
No, not that name was given me at the font,
But 'tis usurp'd ... (*Richard II* IV. i. 254–7)

Both in comedy and tragedy the loss of the name signifies the insecurity of man's rationality and being and becomes an expression of the absurdity of his existence. The comic distance in Shakespeare's farce however, is continued over this crucial issue through the use of the second level of correspondences, that of the Dromios.

The creation of the double set of twins is not just the result of combining two Plautine plays, the *Amphitruo* and the *Brothers Menaechmi*, but a necessary expression of the structural theme which without the clowns' reflection of the main image would become to bold and/or simplistic. Consequently it is Dromio of Ephesus rather than his master who comically expresses the indignation over the loss of their names:

Eph. Ant. What art thou that keep'st me out from the house I owe?
Syr. Dro. The porter for this time, sir, and my name is Dromio.
Eph. Dro. O villain, thou hast stol'n both mine office and my

name;
The one ne'er got me credit, the other mickle blame;
If thou hadst been Dromio to-day in my place,
Thou wouldst have chang'd thy office for an aim, or thy name for an ass. (III. i. 42–7)

Through the clowns, the complexity of correspondence allows the variations on the identity-marriage theme to form an intricate aesthetic pattern of comedy. Central to their existence therefore has to be Nell who proves to be a reflective, though physically distorted, image of Antipholus's Adriana:

> *Syr. Ant.* What woman's man? and how besides thyself?
> *Syr. Dro.* Marry, sir, besides myself, I am due to a woman, one that claims me, one that haunts me, one that will have me.
> *Syr. Ant.* What claim lays she to thee?
> *Syr. Dro.* Marry sir, such claim as you would lay to your horse; and she would have me as a beast, not that I being a beast she would have me, but that she being a very beastly creature lays claim to me.
> *Syr. Ant.* What is she?
> *Syr. Dro.* A very reverend body; ay, such a one as a man may not speak of, without he say 'sir-reverence'; I have but lean luck in the match, and yet is she a wondrous fat marriage.
> *Syr. Ant.* How dost thou mean, a fat marriage?
> *Syr. Dro.* Marry, sir, she's the kitchen wench, and all grease, and I know not what use to put her to but to make a lamp of her, and run from her by her own light. (III. ii. 77-96)

Dromio has to accept Nell for what he sees her to be and then run from her by her own light, just as Antipholus must 'entertain' the 'offered fallacy' in order to escape back to a concrete existence. That fallacy however involves a situation whereby temporarily accepting the negation of one's identity one becomes as a beast; a predicament which the woman has unwittingly forced on the man and yet cannot herself accept. This is true within the concept of the comic structure and by implication through the correspondence of two Antipholuses, in the thematic context of the Antipholus of Ephesus-Adriana marriage. She wishes her husband to be what Dromio comically calls 'a beast', that is something which he is not, an identity totally alien to him. Her love therefore is portrayed as desiring to transform the identity of her partner, a desire which evolves from her natural possessive instincts. It is this expression of possessiveness which becomes yet another implication of the structural theme.

From the opening moments of the play an equation is drawn between possession and existence. At first possession finds its metaphor in gold; Egeon's sentence of death will be repealed only on the ransom of 'a thousand marks' (I. i. 21). We learn too, as we have seen, that his misfortunes accrued because of financial expediency. We discover furthermore, through constant references to the chain, that in Ephesus love, sex and respect are bought with gold, and that without money only punishment and misfortune are to be found. Thus the two Dromios who themselves were bought and are owned by their masters are continually punished for not bringing the correct sums of money to their respective lords. It is not surprising therefore that in this gold-orientated land Adriana sees herself as owning her husband, possessing him as he possesses money whilst he, it is implied, rates her love behind his financial affairs:

Adr. Say, is your tardy master now at hand?
   ... I prithee, is he coming home?
   It seems he hath great care to please his wife.
Eph. Dro. Why, mistress, sure my master is horn-mad.
Adr. Horn-mad, thou villain?
Eph. Dro. I mean not cuckold-mad,
   But sure he is stark mad.
   When I desir'd him to come home to dinner,
   He ask'd me for a thousand marks in gold;
   ''Tis dinner-time,' quoth I; 'my gold,' quoth he;
   'Your meat will burn,' quoth I; 'my gold,' quoth he,
   'Will you come?' quoth I; 'my gold,' quoth he,
   'Where is the thousand marks I gave thee, villain?'
   'The pig,' quoth I, 'is burn'd,'; 'my gold,' quoth he;
   'My mistress, sir ...', quoth I; 'hang up thy mistress;
   I know not thy mistress, out on thy mistress ...'
Luc. Quoth who?
Eph. Dro. Quoth my master;
   'I know,' quoth he, 'no house, no wife, no mistress', ...

> *Adr.* Go back again, thou slave, and fetch him home.
>
> (II. i. 44, 55–71,75)

Dromio of course had been to the wrong Antipholus but the correspondence holds good; the wife being weighed by the gold, the husband being commanded to leave the gold for her companionship.

Identity, marriage, possession are the three issues expounded in the opening scene, clarified as themes by Antipholus of Syracuse's arrival in Ephesus and embellished in an intricate pattern of variations throughout the work leading to a final coda in which the Abbess appears. But does she really, as Evans implies, disrupt the aesthetic pattern?

The concept of the convent and monastery as places of retreat from the complexities of an inexplicable and cruel world was to become a major symbol in the drama of Shakespeare and his contemporaries. Sometimes it was to be employed with startling effect as in the conclusion of Marston's *Antonio's Revenge* or in Hamlet's vicious instructions to Ophelia, but whether here or as in the more conventional use in *The Winter's Tale*, the symbol derived its power from its restorative associations. When all is confusion this archetypal place of retreat allows rest and safety. The priory is the final resort for Antipholus of Syracuse and his servant. Its introduction instructs the audience that the confusions have become so great that all rationality is about to be lost to chaos, unless a traditional answer is found to restore order. The abbess appears and takes control. Instead of entering the debate by concerning herself with the husband, she overtly attempts to change the direction of everyone's thought in order to clarify the true reason for all the problems. Thus instead of condemning Antipholus for his sins she turns to Adriana to instruct her about her judgements and jealousy;

> And thereof came it that the man was mad.
> The venom clamours of a jealous woman
> Poisons more deadly than a mad dog's tooth.
> It seems his sleeps were hinder'd by thy railing,
> And thereof comes it that his head is light.
> Thou say'st his meat was sauc'd with thy upbraidings;
> Unquiet meals make ill digestions ...
> Thou sayest his sports were hinder'd by thy brawls;

Sweet recreation barr'd, what doth ensue
But moody and dull melancholy,
Kinsman to grim and comfortless despair,
And at her heels a huge infectious troop
Of pale distemperatures and foes to life?...
The consequence is then, thy jealous fits
Hath scar'd thy husband from the use of wits.
(v. i. 68–74, 77–82, 85–6)

In one sense only, is the Abbess in as much error as anyone else, the Antipholus she is protecting is not Adriana's husband. Nevertheless her words are valid in iterating the truths which the comic structure has portrayed. If she is believed, all will be restored. The acceptance, however has necessarily to come through the structure itself and it is here by instigating a conventional recognition scene that the Abbess performs the second aspect of her therapeutic role. If not particularly subtle the scene is quite conventional in the Aristotelean context of *anagnorisis* and as such tends to allow a satisfactory and harmonious conclusion to the farce. It may not be that throughout the play we expect the appearance of Egeon's wife in the end but we foresee the necessity of some restoring agent and are not disappointed in the event at finding it to be Emilia. She proves to have been the obvious missing link and her words together with her role of discovery are quite consistent with the progress of the play.

It has been in recent years only that the true implications of farce as an art form have begun to come to light. The very complexity and ingenuity of a premier drama of this kind, which *The Comedy of Errors* inevitably is, illustrate the thematic, social and psychological concerns underlying the artefact. Shakespeare's early comedy is a masterpiece of its peculiar genre and consequently demands to be treated with respect by scholarship and the theatre.[13] If this occurs then its true comic value and potential are realized thus allowing the play to perform its function of joyously and hilariously entertaining its audiences. It is interesting that over the past two decades there have been two major revivals of the play by the Royal Shakespeare Company. But perhaps mention should be made first of an interesting production at Stratford, Connecticut in 1963. This as Harry Levin reports, was notable in that a single actor played both

Antipholuses. In the light of the thematic concerns of the structure such an idea appears immediately attractive but in reality must cause difficulties.[14] If, in farce, the theme depends so much on the structure then an alteration as radical as reducing the two principal parts to one, by employing one actor, forces the theme outside the dramatic form, thus making a directorial thematic commentary on the original play rather than allowing it to develop as it was intended. Shakespeare did not, it seems, want or at least envisage a commentary since he did not include one of his own, as he was later to do with, for example, Feste in *Twelfth Night*. A criticism of this kind about a production naturally treads a sensitive minefield since we find ourselves in the delicate debate concerning the propriety of directorial influence over and interpretation of an established classical text.

Trevor Nunn's production in 1976 met this problem squarely. Realising that farce demands improvisation and the extension of comic business Nunn embellished the work with songs, dances and comic ingenuity so as to realize the vitality behind the original text. At one hilarious moment, for example, Adriana (Judi Dench) appeared at her balcony, stared at the wrong Antipholus below and melodramatically signalled him to her chamber. He and Dromio looked dumbfounded whilst the audience roared. Action here had correctly complemented the text. Trevor Nunn however went further. Although in an interview with *The Times* he asserted that the play had 'no intellectual pretension'[15] he cleverly allowed his musical interpolations to emphasize the drama's key thematic issues whilst the audience sat back to enjoy the songs. Thus between I.i. and I.ii. he introduced a song concerning the need of Egeon for a ransom:

> *Chorus* Beg thou or borrow to make up the sum,
>   make up the sum, make up the sum,
>   Thou art welcome to try.
>   Bring not the money by set of sun,
>   by set of sun,
>   Then ... old man you die,
>   old man you die,
>   old man you die.
> *Girls* Try all the friends thou hast in Ephesus,
> *Proprietor of the Porpentine* Or else your story must end in
>   Ephesus,

Egeon My comfort when your words are done
  My life ends with the evening sun
Chorus Beg thou or borrow to make up the sum,
              make up the sum ...'[16]

The lively chorus moved and swayed around the old man as the song developed. Although they were concerned for him he was to discover that in Ephesus none were quite 'so deaf as us'. The music, the action and the humour naturally allowed the audience to realize that the old man would not die but the words correctly set the tone of the romance. He was in difficulty and so he was to attempt to find friends and save his life although rationally there was little hope of him doing either. The final refrain of the song was 'Then old man you'll die ... so you must try.' It was an interpretative, sensitive and entertaining moment of theatre as the chorus disappeared and the lonely Egeon was led off by a comically officious jailer. Similarly Adriana taking refuge in Campari and soda, and the bespectacled Luciana, attractively peering round her book at the play's action, were given a lengthy, amusing duet and dance routine concerning 'A man is master of his liberty'. Dromio of Syracuse likewise presented a vivacious and humorous song based on II. ii. 63-109, developing the theme 'For there's a time and a season/And for all things/There's a time and a place' whilst Antipholus of Syracuse was permitted to sing of his existential problems, briefly changing the mood by allowing a meditative pause in the midst of the quick-fired activity:

Am I on earth
In heaven or hell?
Do I exist?
Do I appear?
Sleeping, waking,
Sick or well?
Am I bewitched?
Am I here?

In Act IV Scene iv, Pinch led an exciting, anarchic song and dance routine 'Satan come forth', in his attempts to exorcise the devil from Antipholus. This was the magical farce, fun and confusion of Ephesus but within the almost comic chaos the intellectual dimensions of the play were being maintained. Purists might argue that such a course was unnecessary and detrimental to the original text.[17] Audience figures[18] proved however that the show was successful whilst the musical additions remained within the thematic framework of Shakespeare's early farce.

A different kind of interpretative embellishment marked the famous 1962 production in which the director Clifford Williams exploited the comic nature of farce to its physical and intellectual limit. Thus he wrote in a programme note:

> When we speak of farce, we commonly think of curates, trousers, French windows, banana skins, laughter, and incredibility. But farce may be given a dimension and a reality which makes it more fruitful than the most painstaking work of naturalism.
> ... Shakespeare, the dramatist, gives us a crazy though magical Ephesus where men may re-find their brothers and find themselves, and where women may re-find their husbands and learn about themselves. The city and people of Ephesus may be highly improbable, but they are infinitely desirable, a triumph of imagination over life.

To achieve this vision of the play within production Williams expressed the work's relationship with the contemporary popular drama of the Italian *commedia dell'arte*. Consequently the performance was enhanced by an unpretentious, non-intruding use of mime which seemed to develop from the play's structure and promote its fluid progress. His opening balletic sequence and the creation of a silent though very active group of figures observing and reflecting the follies of the stage enabled the structural theme to be kept in focus. The production being staged over a ten year period throughout England, Europe and the United States as well as being televised, was a major success. It was critically acclaimed from the start, Harold Hobson among others, commenting on the way in which the undertones of the work had been sensitively exposed:

> The wild comedy of irrational recognitions is given consistency and a curious force by the suggestion that there is behind

it something vaguely disquieting. (*The Sunday Times*, 16 September 1962)

That 'something' is the very heart of the play's structure and the dramatist's vision, an ability to see and express the comic absurdity of man in the process of living.

2 Dr Faustus

Dr Faustus is a problem play. Its difficulties are many, textual, generic, thematic but in the end they all confront us with the questions of tone and intent. Faustus as a character ostensibly suffers from a massive confidence trick partly of his own making, partly of the devil's. But what is the significance of his 'tragical history' to us the audience? Are we, too, tricked into delusions, false assumptions and erroneous conclusions? Are we in fact asked to take a moral stance, which many critics, directors and audiences in the past have done? Or are we meant to accept a theatrical vision without conscious debate, to understand it as an image of life rather than a discussion of the relationship of the world and the hereafter? A good deal of scholarship has quite rightly been devoted to the medieval and renaissance heritage of the play, its hybrid form and character[1] but within this line of investigation the difficulties of the work have acquired almost monumental proportions. A correct perspective must be kept but it should equally be acknowledged that *Dr Faustus* continues to be performed, almost four hundred years after its initial composition, and to attract modern audiences more than perhaps any other non-Shakespearean play of the Elizabethan era. The work seems to possess therefore some universal quality readily perceptible, if not easily defined, by the twentieth-century spectator. It is this which we must attempt to discover.

Dr Faustus is about sin, death and hell. As such its ambience is naturally derived from Christian tradition and mythology. Devil, fireworks, grotesque visions and comic personifications of evil pervade much of the play in a dramatic tradition dating from *The Castle of Perseverance,* but these theatrical entertainments do not dominate the play's fundamental image. They are what is expected but not what is required for hell to be a reality to a protagonist who confronted by a devil, still maintains, 'I think hell's a fable.' Mephostophilis's reply however crystallizes the truth to come, 'Ay, think so still, till experience change thy mind.'[2] Hell is a state of mind, a realization of one's experiences, not a chamber of unspeakable tortures, 'Hell hath no limits, nor is circumscrib'd/In one self place, but where we are is hell,/And where hell is, there must we ever be' (Sc. v. 122–4). As such the hell described beneath the medieval trappings of this play is not dissimilar to a vision still created on the modern stage in post-war Europe. Thus an affinity may be descried between the Faustian experience and that for example, of Sartre's hell-bound figures in *In Camera* where at the beginning of the play the Valet humorously dismisses Garcia's childish fantasies of physical pain:

> *Garcia* ... I certainly didn't expect – this! You know what they tell us down there?
> *Valet* What about?
> *Garcia* About this – er – residence.
> *Valet* Really, sir, how could you believe such cock-and-bull stories? Told by people who'd never have set foot here. For, of course, if they had ...
> *Garcia* Quite so. *[Both laugh. Abruptly the laugh dies from Garcia's face.]* But, I say, where are the instruments of torture?
> *Valet* The what?
> *Garcia* The racks and red-hot pincers and all the other paraphernalia?
> *Valet* Ah, you must have your little joke, sir!
> *Garcia* My little joke? Oh, I see. No, I wasn't joking.[3]

Sartre's hell is one that is gradually perceived by those experiencing it. At first it is imagined in terms of expectation and thus, once physical torture is dismissed, Garcia assumes a psychic nightmare:

> ... that bronze contraption on the mantelpiece, that's another story. I suppose there will be times when I stare my eyes out at it. Stare my eyes out – see what I mean? ... All right, let's put our cards on the table. I assure you I'm quite conscious of my position. Shall I tell you what it feels like? A man's drowning, choking, sinking by inches, till only his eyes are just above water. And what does he see? A bronze atrocity by – what's the fellow's name – Barbedienne. A collector's piece.

Like a nightmare. That's the idea, isn't it? ... I've a shrewd notion of what's coming to me, so don't you boast you've caught me off guard. I'm facing up to the situation, facing up. *[He starts pacing the room again.]* So that's that; no toothbrush. And no bed either. One never sleeps, I take it? (p.109)

Garcia's introduction to hell, set in a Second Empire-style drawing room, is one of assumptions, questions and even ironic disappointments as indeed were those of Faustus in the former play:

Faustus ... yet fain would I have a book wherein I might behold all spells and incantations, that I might raise up spirits when I please.
Mephostophilis Here they are in this book. *[There turn to them.]*
Faustus Now would I have a book wherein I might see all characters of planets of the heavens, that I might know their motions and dispositions.
Mephostophilis Here they are, too. *[Turn to them.]*
Faustus Nay, let me have one book more, and then I have done, wherein I might see all plants, herbs, and trees that grow upon the earth.
Mephostophilis Here they be.
Faustus O, thou art deceived.
Mephostophilis Tut, I warrant thee. *[Turn to them. Exeunt.]*
(Sc. v. 166–79)

The probing, the questioning, the false assumptions, the ironic disappointments are a part of the Satanic experience, an experience which devoid of its mythological terminology proves to be a state of selfish being, self-imposed isolation in what is potentially a social context. Thus in *In Camera* once Garcia is joined by Inez and Estelle, a vision is drawn whereby no common bond can be formed by the three isolated figures. In desperation they realize the effect of their hell but not its cause. 'Hell is other people' (p.166). The reverse is true; hell is oneself unable to give, to care for or communicate with others.

Such a situation is Faustus's only desire from the beginning of Marlowe's play. For the sake of fame this arrogant doctor wishes for isolation, longs for an unnatural detachment since within that lies renown and glory:

> Are not thy bills hung up as monuments,
> Whereby whole cities have escap'd the plague
> And thousand desperate maladies been cur'd?
> Yet art thou still but Faustus, and a man.
> Couldst thou make men to live eternally
> Or being dead raise them to life again,
> Then this profession were to be esteem'd. (Sc. i. 20–26)

The author's concern in this great soliloquy is not to denigrate ambition but to expose the stultifying effect of its abuse. Faustus from the beginning is presented as an icon of sterility, misquoting Aristotle, misunderstanding scripture, misdirecting his intellectual potential. The opening of the play presents an introductory tableau to a scene of hell, and as the play progresses we are to discover that although the plot traces 'Faustus' fortunes, good or bad' (Prologue 8) until he is dragged down to Satan's mythological dungeon, the iconic, thematic vision throughout is in fact one of the Satanic experience.

On one level of the play we may be concerned with such questions as whether Faustus will repent or not, and maintain our interest in them through the course of the narrative, but on another we are ever acutely conscious of the different faces being shown by Faustus. There is a disquieting ambiguity in his presence since, as with Dorian Gray in Wilde's tale, the audience is always aware of the grotesque portrait hidden away in the attic room. We realize that from the moment of signing the diabolic pact Faustus has committed himself not merely to the mythological hell after death, but to a living reality. His contract is a marriage to corruption, degradation and stagnation. Thus M.C. Bradbrook instructively tells us:

> When Faustus sold his soul, he obliterated his ability to possess a past, since every action that fell behind him into the past pushed him nearer his final end; nor could he look at the future, but only at the present. His magic annihilated Space, but his bondage contracted Time; the last hour as it closes in, shows him only where he is, and where in effect he had been living for four-and-twenty years.[4]

The midnight hour at which Faustus signs his covenant with the devil corresponds to the stroke of twelve he hears twenty-four years later. In a hellish sense both moments are the same, since from signing to dying Faustus achieves no spiritual development. His soul stagnates with his sin, although his body lives on for the duration allotted. Consequently his words, on putting his name to the deed are ironically the first and yet final expression of his evil:

> *Consummatum est:* the bill is ended,
> And Faustus hath bequeath'd his soul to Lucifer.
> But what is this inscription on mine arm?
> *Homo fuge!* Whither should I fly?
> If unto God, he'll throw me down to hell. –
> My senses are deceiv'd, here's nothing writ. –
> Oh yes, I see it plain; even here is writ,
> *Homo fuge!* Yet shall not Faustus fly. (Sc. v. 74–81)

Succinctly this speech reveals the whole nature of his damnation: the ironic blasphemous echo of Christ's dying words on the cross, the ability to see the need to fly from sin but the inability to recognize and accept Christ's saving grace brought to the world on the occasion of those words, and the foolish reconciliation of himself to a needless fate, 'Yet shall not Faustus fly'.[5] In total the play is an embellishment of this moment, sometimes conducted comically as in the sub-plots or the Papal episodes, sometimes pathetically as in the sensual scene with Helen and sometimes tragically as in the final soliloquy. Whichever, the irony of the Faustian predicament is constantly apparent. The play operates therefore in an almost metaphysical way, being an example of the ingenious manner by which the English renaissance wits were able to juxtapose varieties of images, situations and even genres (comic, tragic, pathetic) in close proximity with one another so as to express a central theme or issue.[6] *Dr Faustus* becomes a grotesque tableau of the protagonist's living death. Before him pass his ephemeral achievements, his futile successes with Pope, Emperor or minion, his sensual excesses with concubine, devil or abstraction, but in the end all these distinct images form the total effect of the icon, the frightened yet arrogant man, knowing his sin, aware of the possibility of its relief yet impotent in action. Here lies the strength of the play's seemingly diverse elements:

> Curs'd be the parents that engender'd me!
> No, Faustus, curse thyself, curse Lucifer
> That hath depriv'd thee of the joys of heaven.
> *The clock striketh twelve.*
> O, it strikes, it strikes! Now, body, turn to air,
> Or Lucifer will bear thee quick to hell! (Sc. xix, 180–4)

Humour, pathos, tragedy in the final analysis fail to dominate. There is merely confirmation of the protagonist's futility in the face of his predicament:

> Stand still, you ever-moving spheres of heaven,
> That time may cease, and midnight never come;
> Fair nature's eye, rise, rise again, and make
> Perpetual day; or let this hour be but
> A year, a month, a week, a natural day,
> That Faustus may repent and save his soul.
> *O lente lente currite noctis equi!* (Sc. xix 136–42)

The chilling irony of these words is apparent not only in the Ovidian echo, which has often been noted, but in the final reaffirmation of the Faustian evil, a sin which in itself has prohibited the natural course of time for the protagonist's spiritual development.

Faustus therefore is an icon of evil presented to an audience to perform a natural symbolic function, a representation, in M.C. Bradbrook's words of 'the ideals or fears of a community'.[7] Whether that community is largely Christian as in Marlowe's own day or largely secular, but retaining a cultural base derived from the Christian tradition as in our own, does not really matter since the dilemma presented seems to have a timeless significance. Consequently in the relationship of the icon to the mixed genres of the artefact an affinity between Marlowe's play and modern theatre is easily discovered. It has already been noted how Sartre in *In Camera* is able to mix moods, comic, ironic, pathetic, in his introductory depiction of the stagnant image, but this methodology finds an even more pertinent expression in later French drama such as Ionesco's *Exit the King*.

The parallels between this play and the renaissance stage are not fortuitous, Ionesco being particularly indebted for his inspiration to *Everyman* and Shakespeare's *Richard II*. Nevertheless it is remarkable how parallels between this quite recent work (1962) and that of Marlowe helps to put the earlier drama into focus.[8] The comic-horrific mood of the absurd portrait of King Berenger's palace environment is the essence of the play's *modus operandi*. Farce prevails even though Berenger is facing the moment of his death, announced to him over and over again by a larger-than-life doctor, a tin soldier and a rather macabre, officious wife:

Doctor If you look through this telescope, which can see through roofs and walls, you will notice a gap in the sky that used to house the Royal Constellation. In the annals of the universe his majesty has been entered as deceased.
Guard The King is dead! Long live the King!
Queen Marguerite [*to the Guard*] Idiot! Can't you keep quiet!
Doctor He is, indeed, far more dead than alive.
King I'm not.[9]

In this representative exchange Ionesco's peculiar tone in methodology is apparent. Although the subject, the King's death, is being seriously considered by the play it is done so through the comic guise of gross exaggeration, a method employed continually by Marlowe although in his case through the expedience of the sub-plots. Consequently, as has been amply shown by Robert Ornstein, it is in the relationship of the comic scenes to the protagonist that much of the poignancy of the Marlovian drama is found, the clowns showing through correspondence that:

... it does not matter whether one sells one's soul for infinite power or for belly cheer. Both transactions are ridiculous, the first even more than the second because it is far less realistic.[10]

Thus the mixture of perspective helps to define the centrality of the dominating icon or symbol crystallizing the audience's response towards it. By the time we reach Berenger's actual moment of death in Ionesco's play, we are prepared to see it as the moment of synthesis for all that has preceded it, and as such we neither question its validity nor scorn its exaggeration but accept it totally in its embracing iconism. Like Faustus, Berenger, realizing his total isolation wishes that time might cease for ever:

No-one can or will help me. And *I* can't help myself. O help me, sun! Sun, chase away the shadows and hold back the night! Sun, sun illumine every tomb, shine into every hole and corner, every nook and cranny! Creep deep inside me! Ah! Now my feet are turning cold. Come and warm me! pierce my body, steal beneath my skin, and blaze into my eyes! Restore their failing light, and let me see, see, see! Sun, sun, will you miss me? Good little sun, protect me! And if you're in need of some small sacrifice, then parch and wither up the world. Let every human creature die provided that *I* can live for ever, even alone in a limitless desert. I'll come to terms with solitude. I'll keep alive the memory of others, and I'll miss them quite sincerely. But I can live in the void, in a vast and airy wasteland. It's better to miss one's friends than to be missed oneself. Besides, one never is. Light of our days, come and save me! (pp. 51–2)

The icon here, of total selfishness impotently crying to external powers but unable to admit social, and thereby individual responsibility, is plainly a descendant of Marlowe's hero[11] and as such illustrates the reason for his continued stage success. Like Berenger, Faustus can still be seen as a dominant symbol of a universal social fear, that of the inconsequence of existence. He is an icon of futility and as such performs the complex role of a 'true symbol' as explained in the modern theatre by Peter Brook:

...a true symbol is specific, it is the only form a certain truth can take. The two men waiting by a stunted tree, the man recording himself on tape, the two men marooned in a tower, the woman buried to her waist in sand, the parents in the dustbins, the three heads in the urns: these are pure inventions, fresh images sharply defined – and they stand on the stage as objects. They are theatre machines. People smile at them, but they hold their ground: they are critic-proof. We get nowhere if we expect to be told what they mean, yet each one has a relation with us we can't deny.[12]

To this list is naturally added the man huddled over parchment, endlessly signing his name in his own blood whilst looking to the heavens in the anguish of a dying moment. This is Faustus, Marlowe's absurd hero, 'critic-proof' perhaps but certainly still able to hold his theatrical ground.

Nevertheless, despite its inherent modernity *Dr Faustus* has offered a severe challenge to theatre directors over the years and none more so than in the past two decades. Often the tendency has been to become over-interpretative. Directors instinctively understanding a major aspect of the Marlovian design, have been prone to emphasize it to the detriment of the work's thematic balance. Thus the renowned Polish director Jerzy Grotowski rearranged the scene sequence of the play so as to present a montage illustrative of his personal concept of Faustus as a secular saint fighting against the tyranny of God. He explained his ideas in a note on the production:

> Faustus is a saint and his saintliness shows itself as an absolute desire for pure truth. If the saint is to become one with his sainthood, he must rebel against God, Creator of the world, because the laws of the world are traps contradicting morality and truth ... Whatever we do – good or bad – we are damned. The saint is not able to accept as his model this God who ambushes man. God's laws are lies, He spies on the dishonor in our souls the better to damn us. Therefore, if one wants sainthood, one must be against God.[13]

The implication must be that an identification of the director and the Faustian role was taking place in this production. By looking at the play through Faustus's eyes Grotowski, although not altering one word of the text, created a new work which did not have to concern itself with a sixteenth-century audience's knowledge of the relationship of mercy and justice in the Christian tradition. Faustus had become the revolutionary easily recognizable to a modern audience but he was now Grotowski's creation, not Marlowe's, and had to be appreciated in such terms.

John Barton's 1974 production for the Royal Shakespeare Company was deliberately intellectual. This was a play about a scholar and thus Faustus's sin was contained within the mind. The complete action took place within his study, the claustrophobic set littered with the paraphernalia of the student, visually symbolising the protagonist's mental state. In the midst of this Ian McKellen portrayed a highly intense Faustus creating his own private sinful world. His spirits, including Helen of

Troy, were figments of the imagination, portrayed as puppets, whilst Emrys James's Mephostophilis looked on as a languid ghost haunting room and protagonist but resigned that even this task was a part of his own private hell. There was little humour in the production, the majority of the comic episodes being excised since, as Mr Barton explained in a programme note, he just did not find them funny:

> Though in theory the sub-plots provide a complementary comment on the main action by showing the abuse of necromantic powers in trivial pranks, in practice they tend to trivialise the tone of the play itself. At least, that has been the experience of myself and many others on seeing the play in the theatre.

To compensate for the lines lost and to reinforce his interpretation the director consequently included information and episodes from Marlowe's source, the *English Faust Book*, and added approximately five hundred and fifty new lines written by himself. It would be difficult to say that such an action totally betrayed the original's intent as the texts we have are so uncertain but we might question whether in focusing so strongly on the intensity of the sin, Mr Barton lost the ambiguity that is at the heart of the play. There was an exterior almost scientific analysis about the performance which culminated in Faustus dying from a series of painfully acute heart attacks. Naturalistically this may have made sense for the twentieth-century but it tended to force an interpretation rather than allow the myth to work in its own terms.[14] Earlier RSC productions showed this to be possible.

In 1970 Gareth Morgan presented the work for the RSC's *Theatregoround* in a production which aimed to harmonize many of the play's seemingly diverse aspects. In this shoestring performance the fifty or so parts in the play were taken by just twelve actors on a rudimentary set consisting principally of black studio-workshop boxes. The object was to stimulate the imagination to the ambiguities of the work and the Faustian predicament, with the result that some neat parallels were suggested. Thus the late Clement McCallin for example, played both Lucifer and the Pope, a device which naturally created in an entertaining manner, an impression of the extent of Faustus's delusions. Although by no means unanimously acclaimed by the critics the performance was competent within its financial limits and challenging in its appeal.

Even more successful, however, was Clifford Williams's production of 1968 which correctly exploited various elements of the complex image with a consistent emphasis, thus allowing one aspect to balance or sharply focus another. Nigel Alexander has recorded in particular the way in which Williams managed to convey the historical emblems of the work in a timeless manner. Thus the appearance of the seven deadlies with elongated limbs correctly conveyed the Marlovian image to the modern audience:

> [The] suggestion of a threatening presence forecasting a desperate future was ... achieved by the weird skeletal figures employed.... They are 'unhistorical' in the sense that they do not resemble contemporary depictions of the seven deadly sins but they are also 'historical' in the sense that they convey to a modern audience the imminent threat of death and decay contained in the biblical text which Faustus has already dismissed.[15]

Eric Porter as Faustus found a consistent through-line for the part, enjoying the comedy which Williams slickly presented with the skill of a farceur. The protagonist enjoyed the fun, joyously contemplated the grotesque peep show of the seven deadlies and became bewitchingly enraptured by the vision of a naked Helen of Troy passing slowly across the rear of the stage, but he also displayed a simultaneous horror of his deeds. The ambiguity of the Marlovian balance was thus maintained creating an appropriate dramatic tension. All came together in the final scene with the soliloquy delivered by Porter with expert timing. Yet as the dreadful minute arrived, nothing happened. Gradually Faustus realized that he had escaped as Nigel Alexander recounts:

> After a long moment Faustus raised his head and looked around the totally empty stage. He started to laugh. As he reached the hysteria of relief, the back wall of the stage gave way and fell forward in sections revealing an ominous red glow and a set of spikes like the dragon's teeth of the Siegfried Line. The denizens of hell emerged with a kind of slow

continuous shuffle until Faustus was surrounded by a circle of these skeletal figures – including the seven deadly sins.[16]

The laughter had ceased. Faustus was damned and his shrieks of despair rang out as he was dragged to the fires beyond. The walls of the study then reassembled leaving all as it was, with the notable quiet exception of the protagonist. Myth had come alive on stage allowing the medievalism and the modernity of this renaissance work to fuse. The Faustian mind and body had indulged in the grotesque visions not only of Marlowe but of both Hieronymous Bosch and Salvador Dali and had received their necessary and comprehensible reward.

The most recent revival of the play was presented in London in 1980, at the Lyric Studio, Hammersmith and subsequently at the Fortune Theatre in a production by Christopher Fettes. As with Gareth Morgan's production there was only a small cast with six of the actors taking numerous parts. James Aubrey played Faustus and Patrick Magee, Mephostophilis. Magee's presence influenced the complete production. His doleful sunken eyes within his dachshund face, his fatigued step and his chilling intoned voice with its heavy stress on final syllables, produced the resignation of evil. Faustus's enthusiasm was an absurdity confronted with this sadly-deep old man. Indeed one wondered how Faustus could embrace sin when early in the play Valdes and Cornelius appeared as sickly degenerates. They were like characters from a Beckett play, the ashen Valdes asthmatically coughing next to the impotent, blind Cornelius confined to a wheel chair. Who, one wondered, would go to dinner with such creatures as these? The set was dominated by a long refectory table at which the scholars read, these students in black becoming the voices of the good and bad angels. The Chorus also in black was more decadent than moralistic, smoking a cigarella as he recounted the story with an almost Mephostophi-lean resignation. The fall of Faustus was not to be a monumen-tally tragic affair but a minor matter-of-fact story in the history of a rather dull world. A white linen traverse gauze behind the table allowed a further section to the stage in which the dumb shows were presented, bright lights illuminating the figures through the texture of the cloth, whilst loud music ranging from Wagner to contemporary often sounded, compelling the audi-ence to think and listen. Alexander appeared behind this gauze as did Helen, the latter being portrayed by a boy. Wearing a white linen trouser costume with gold fastenings around the ankles and the back slit to the waist, this Helen was exquisitely decadent. She moved slowly head high, mesmeric eyes penetrating in the steady stare of something from another world. Faustus was a slave to her but the audience was far from convinced of her beauty and was rightly uneasy at her appearance. Much of the comic business was again cut but the Pope did appear and was cleverly cast as a dwarf. Pompously strutting and arrogantly mounting his throne from Bruno's back he gave the air of an absurd little man dressed with proud authority. The Faustian tricks reduced him to a sniffling child. A similar irony to that found in Gareth Morgan's production was achieved with the dwarf also playing the part of Beelzebub. Aubrey's Faustus, intent on sin from the play's opening wearied rather than aged as the play progressed, a glut of sin leading to his unemotional death.

Fettes's production as with Williams's, twelve years earlier, proved *Dr Faustus* to be applicable for the modern stage. But whereas Williams did this through colour and emotion, Fettes realized the intellectual tradition of Barton and Morgan. He produced a stagnant, claustrophobic Faustus but still allowed the ironies to suggest themselves to the audience. As these productions proved, *Dr Faustus* is a difficult play but it is within its problematic structure and ambiguous tenor that the height of its achievement lies. It demands to be approached head on and accepted in the context of its complex image, a disparate and yet unified aesthetic pattern which proves to be both the strength and appeal of its central icon.

3 The Revenger's Tragedy

In 1936 G. Wilson Knight wrote in *The Principles of Shakespearian Production*:

> The producer should be aware of the play's metaphysical core; that is, of its wholeness. He must not consider *Hamlet* and *Macbeth* as merely good stories with occasional 'dramatic situations'; no modern producer would blunder like that with a Galsworthy play. Close intellectual interpretation must come first, and interpretation involves numerous subtleties. But the closest attention to details, unless also vitalized by a sense of some unifying idea, will prove fruitless.[1]

For the director and critic of *The Revenger's Tragedy* it is this 'unifying idea' or 'metaphysical core' which often seems to appear so elusive. Tourneur's play[2] defies traditional attempts to discover what Stanislavsky termed the 'super-objective' since it constantly employs modes of irony and moral commentary which naturally undercut developments in plot and characterization.[3] Its figures are deliberately dehumanised in its morality tradition[4] and yet its seemingly thematic purpose is often frustrated by what appears to be contrivance and mechanical invention. Thus the preservation of Castiza's chastity can be regarded as inconsistent with the conduct of the rest of the play in which the two similar exemplars of virtue, Gloriana and Antonio's wife, have been destroyed by the evils of the court. Similarly objections can be made to Vindice's fatal confession since it may appear ridiculously contrived in contrast with the Machiavellian skills that he has displayed throughout. Such inconsistencies have led some critics, such as Madeleine Doran to make adverse comments:

> In *The Revenger's Tragedy* ...[the dramatist] keeps a motive

from Senecan tragedy, but discards the machinery and drains the motive of its implications; he substitutes incompletely a Christian scheme of ethics, hence ultimately puzzles our response to his protagonist.[5]

This criticism holds true if in a Stanislavskian manner we attempt to find a through line of action towards a superobjective by means of plot, characterization or sustained didacticism. Tourneur's methodology defies such rigid classifications. As with all good plays a superobjective or metaphysical core can be found but it has to be sought for in the complex interaction of its events and characters displayed not so much in linear terms but exemplified through the art of contradiction, contrast, alienation and juxtaposition. To discover how this is achieved we may examine three specific areas: the portrayal of Vindice; the correspondences between Gloriana, Antonio's wife and Castiza, and the relationship of the minor figures Spurio, Ambitioso, Supervacuo and Junior Brother, to the activities and methodology of the principal action.

R.A. Foakes has already noted that from the start of the play Vindice's motives for revenge are placed in an ambiguous light. His opening soliloquy describing Gloriana compromises his sincerity in that it appreciates 'her beauty according to the way it provoked lust in men':[6]

>   ... 'twas a face
> So far beyond the artificial shine
> Of any woman's bought complexion,
> That the uprightest man (if such there be
> That sin but seven times a day) broke custom,
> And made up eight with looking after her (I. i. 20–5)

Such an attitude encourages the audience to regard Vindice as being a part of the corrupt environment he is proposing to destroy. As the play progresses this initial hint is gradually developed into a full statement culminating in the repulsive manner by which he murders the duke. The avenger's desire to kill his victim by smearing the masked skull with poison operates on two ironic levels.[7] The first, like the execution of the king in Marlowe's *Edward II* is at the duke's expense. He dies as he has lived, in the debauchery of his lust. The second however involves

Vindice and Gloriana. She died because she refused to sleep with the duke, refused that is to embrace him in lust. Vindice wishes to avenge this murder and yet does so by actually prostituting Gloriana's skull. He consequently violates her remains in a manner in which she refused to be employed in life.[8] It is a moment of supreme irony fittingly presented by the dramatist with intense theatricality. The duke makes his advances in a darkened, incensed chamber:

> *Duke* How sweet can a duke breathe? Age has no fault.
>   Pleasure should meet in perfumed mist.
>   Lady, sweetly encounter'd; I came from court,
>   I must be bold with you. *[Kisses the skull.]* O, What's this O!
> *Vindice* Royal villain, white devil!
> *Duke*   O!
> *Vindice*   Brother –
>   Place the torch here, that his affrighted eyeballs
>   May start into those hollows. Duke, dost know
>   Yon dreadful vizard? View it well; 'tis the skull
>   Of Gloriana, whom thou poisonedst last. (III. v. 143–51)

Gloriana is forced to embrace in death that which she refused to admit to her body in life. It is an ironically horrifying moment exposing the perversity of Vindice's sadism. As such it naturally and deliberately repulses any sympathetic engagement between the hero and the audience. Yet for the moral balance of the play as a whole[9] the creation of an unsympathetic protagonist presents immense problems. If the audience is to be antagonized by Vindice's overall conduct how can the dramatist employ the character's centrality in the work to give a moral alternative to the decadence portrayed? Tourneur's answer is to capitalize on the very alienating factors which naturally repulse us. He denies audience empathy through the use of such effects as the pun within the irony itself and the creation of the protagonist's twin persona, Piato.[10] Thus for example, just before the ironic moment when the duke kisses the skull Tourneur relieves any emotional tension within the audience by allowing Vindice to make a humorous pun on the word 'grave' and by giving him a brief aside commenting on the situation:

> *Vindice* ... Your grace knows now what you have to do;

> sh' has somewhat a grave look with her, but –
> *Duke* I love that best; conduct her.
> *Vindice [Aside]*   Have at all!
> *Duke* In gravest looks the greatest faults seem less.
>   Give me that sin that's rob'd in holiness. (III. v. 136–41)

The dramatist here humorously builds irony upon irony even to the extent of having the Duke accurately describe the nature of Vindice's act. It is a sin robed in the 'holiness' or the excuse of vengeance. Through it he engages the audience's intellect allowing us to comprehend the full enormity of the ensuing evils. A similarly important alienating device is produced through the close relationship Tourneur allows between Vindice and his disguise as Piato. It is made clear that we are constantly meant to see elements of Vindice within Piato and vice versa. Thus when dressed as Piato, as the text informs us (IV. ii. 26) Vindice continues to employ his own voice.[11] The roles however, are not synonymous. Tourneur clearly wished to allow enough distinction between the actor and his role for Vindice periodically to step outside of his part in order to present a moral commentary on the actions that he is in the process of committing. A principal example of this occurs with the scene in which Vindice tempts Gratiana to prostitute Castiza. In the role of Piato he conducts this spiritual rape of his mother with all the eloquence he can muster:

> Would I be a poor, dejected, scorn'd of greatness,
> Swept from the palace, and see other daughters
> Spring with the dew o' th' court, having mine own
> So much desir'd and lov'd – by the duke's son?
> No, I would raise my state upon her breast,
> And call her eyes my tenants; I would count
> My yearly maintenance upon her cheeks,
> Take coach upon her lip, and all her parts
> Should keep men after men, and I would ride
> In pleasure upon pleasure.
> You took great pains for her, once when it was,
> Let her requite it now, though it be but some:
> You brought her forth, she well may bring you home.
>   (II. i. 91–103)

– and yet immediately as Vindice comments on his own progress and activity:

> *Gratiana*   O heavens!
>   This overcomes me.
> *Vindice [Aside]*   Not, I hope, already!
> *Gratiana [Aside]*   It is too strong for me, men know that know us:
>   We are so weak, their words can overthrow us.
>   He touch'd me nearly, made my virtues bate,
>   When his tongue struck upon my poor estate.
> *Vindice [Aside]*   I e'en quake to proceed, my spirit turns edge;
>   I fear me she's unmother'd, yet I'll venture.
> *That woman is all male, whom none can enter.* (II. i. 104–12)

The result is a classic example of alienation. The audience involved with the eloquence of temptation is distanced from it by melodramatic asides which force an intellectual appraisal of the total situation. The result is that all the seemingly contradictory moral statements being made can be held simultaneously in a single theatrical image. Thus we visualize the unnatural degeneracy of a mother ready to prostitute her child for wealth and position, remember the vulnerability of the daughter herself and the weakness of the female sex attacked by the strength and wiles of the male, condemn the son's very act of temptation and yet possibly laugh at the vigour of his grotesque ambiguity, all in a moment. In this way Vindice is therefore presented as a deliberately ambivalent figure created to conduct acts of degeneracy and simultaneously to provide the stimulus for the audience's moral awareness of his evil.[12]

In marked contrast to Vindice are a group of women who tend to correspond one with each other: Castiza, Gloriana and Antonio's wife. Throughout the play chastity, as we have seen, is constantly violated by both the court and the avenger, to the extent that even the grave is abused. Thus Gloriana dies because of the advances of the lascivious as does Antonio's wife after she has suffered the indignity of Junior Brother's violence. Her husband records the event:

> Then, with a face more impudent than his vizard,
> He harried her amidst a throng of panders

That live upon damnation of both kinds,
And fed the ravenous vulture of his lust
(O death to think on't!). She, her honour forc'd,
Deem'd it a nobler dowry for her name
To die with poison than to live with shame. (I. iv. 41–7)

This account of the lady's death comes in the concluding scene of the first act, and complements the view already illustrated by Vindice's opening soliloquy and Junior Brother's ineffectual trial, that at this court chastity is something to be destroyed either by lust or by poison. The next act opens however with the appearance of Castiza proclaiming the hard but determined reality of her name, chastity:

How hardly shall that maiden be beset,
Whose only fortunes are her constant thoughts;
That has no other child's-part but her honour,
That keeps her low and empty in estate.
Maids and their honours are like poor beginners;
Were not sin rich, there would be few sinners.
Why had not virtue a revenue well,
I know the cause, 'twould have impoverish'd hell. (II. i. 1–8)

A relationship is obviously implied between the three women and therefore in the conduct of the narrative, this speech exposes Castiza's vulnerability. With theatrical skill Tourneur immediately capitalizes on this fact and yet simultaneously frustrates its logic. Dondolo, the bald fool, is introduced to taunt the maid with foul innuendo:

Dondolo   Madonna, there is one, as they say a thing of flesh and blood, a man I take him by his beard, that would very desirously mouth to mouth with you.
Castiza   What's that?
Dondolo   Show his teeth in your company.
Castiza   I understand thee not.
Dondolo   Why, speak with you, Madonna.
Castiza   Why, say so madman, and cut off a great deal of dirty way; had it not been better spoke in ordinary words, that one would speak with me? (II. i. 10–19)

Despite the inherent weakness of her moral stance Castiza strongly rebukes Dondolo, though it has little effect, as she does Vindice in his appearance as a messenger from Lussurioso:

> *Castiza*   Whence this?
> *Vindice*   O, from a dear and worthy friend, Mighty!
> *Castiza*   From whom?
> *Vindice*   The duke's son
> *Castiza*   Receive that!
>   [*A box o' th'ear to her brother.*]
> I swore I'd put anger in my hand,
> And pass the virgin limits of myself,
> To him that next appear'd in that base office,
> To be his sin's attorney. (II. i. 29–35)

Though in an inherently weak position Castiza paradoxically shows that the strength of her morality lies in the firmness and pride which destroyed the lives of the corresponding women. Throughout the drama she continues to display their obstinacy in honour even to the extent of teaching her mother a moral lesson which if considered in terms of the plot alone, might sound absurdly ridiculous:

> ... no tongue has force to alter me from honest.
> If maidens would, men's words could have no power;
> A virgin honour is a crystal tower,
> Which, being weak, is guarded with good spirits;
> Until she basely yields, no ill inherits. (IV. iv. 150–4)

The conduct of the court illustrates that obstinacy in itself will not protect the virgin. She is vulnerable despite her prayers. But if she keeps true to her beliefs even though she dies, even though her corpse is prostituted in death, she will have achieved something that none of her violators can imagine. 'No ill inherits' her Christian honour, her positive attitude to living. Though dead she triumphs with the 'good spirits' that 'guard her' since through the honoured deaths of Gloriana and Antonio's wife it is implied by correspondence that Castiza has also come to terms with that dominant symbol of the play, the skull. For them death is an irrelevancy not in the ironic context of Vindice's words –

> see, ladies, with false forms
> You deceive men, but cannot deceive worms. (III. v. 97–8)[13]

– but in the Christian stoicism of their determination and their very existence. Castiza does not die but lives as a testimony to positive moral values.

The words of Castiza therefore encapsulate the characteristics of Gloriana and Antonio's wife and as such form a moral counterpoint to the activities of the Duke, Lussurioso and Vindice. At the other end of the scale however, lie Spurio and the Duchess's sons. Their music, if such it be, is one of discord and cacophony which grotesquely imitates the evil preoccupation of the principal characters. It adds a further dimension to the total composition of the play re-inforcing our understanding of the Duke's world as one devoid of stability. Spurio, for example, displays a perverse morbidity over the very process of his procreation:

> Faith, if the truth were known, I was begot
> After some gluttonous dinner, some stirring dish
> Was my first father, when deep healths went round,
> And ladies' cheeks were painted red with wine,
> Their tongues as short and nimble as their heels,
> Uttering words sweet and thick; and when they rose,
> Were merrily dispos'd to fall again, –
> In such a whisp'ring and withdrawing hour,
> When base male-bawds kept sentinel at stair head,
> Was I stol'n softly ... (I. ii. 180–9)[14]

The renaissance stage-bastards of course, like those of Shakespeare's *King John* or *King Lear*, had the grievance of lost inheritance close to their hearts. Spurio is such a man reflecting in his hatred the decadence and depravity of a society devoid of roots or morality; a world based not on sexual love but on casual drunken flurries of the blood. Junior Brother rapes Antonio's wife for no reason but that of 'flesh and blood/What should move men unto woman else?'(I. ii. 48–9) The Duchess will sleep with bastard; the bastard with Duchess, merely from motives of revenge. These characters therefore create the ambience of moral sterility that pervades the domestic environment of the court but expands outwards[15] to make even the rule of law ineffectual and futile. The trial of Junior Brother is stage-managed from the start. Outward shows of respectability are created as a substitute for the real foundation of society. With law perverted no protection can be given to the individual and whether guilty or not execution becomes a matter of chance. Lussurioso happens to escape whilst Junior Brother is executed. The whole business is not one of justice but of whim and coincidence. The plans of Supervacuo and Ambitioso may succeed or they may not succeed since their victories are as immoral as themselves. Thus everyone chases round after everyone else attempting to hit a specified target but usually missing, thus killing someone else by accident. In the end all are slaughtered in a scene of absurd self-destructive butchery:

Supervacuo Then I proclaim myself; now am I duke.
Ambitioso   Thou duke? Brother, thou liest. *[Stabs Supervacuo.]*
Spurio   Slave, so dost thou. *[Stabs Ambitioso.]*
4th Noble Base villain, hast thou slain my lord and master?
                                   [Stabs Spurio.]
                 (v. iii. 53–5)

The scene is farcical but it is the logical outcome of a world which has abolished law, since it is an expression of total anarchy.[16]

The Revenger's Tragedy thus has to be seen as composite image, comparable with a painting which becomes more intelligible as we stand back from it to view it in its totality. Central to it are mechanisms of decadence, the abused phallus, the rotting skull, the corruption of power and law which culminate in anarchic destruction. In contrast there are the innocent victims drawn slightly but still apparent in the light of truth and stability. Yet foreshadowing all is the disturbing presence of the misguided, perverted, cynical avenger overviewing the total destruction that he has perpetrated. But as he is led off to execution Tourneur maintains the ambiguity that has dominated his play. Vindice's death is not allowed to symbolize the restoration of normal moral behaviour since uncertainty is permitted to surround his sentence. As has often been illustrated, Antonio judges Vindice from a situation of self-preservation, 'Such an old man as he;/

You that would murder him would murder me.' (v. iii. 104–5) Consequently he adds the final touch of irony to the picture. Do his words imply that he will prove to be just as decadent a ruler as those who have been destroyed, or is one to infer that at least he has the strength of his newly gained office to make decisions that will maintain order by eliminating the agents of anarchy? Tourneur does not tell us but merely allows the words and sentence to stand as a final question in a complex work of art.

The response to *The Revenger's Tragedy* by the twentieth-century theatre has been significant in its success. The first professional production since the seventeenth-century was at the Pitlochry Festival Theatre in 1965 directed by Brian Shelton with Brian Harrison as Vindice. First and foremost Mr Shelton saw the theatrical potential of a vital text which seemed to gain its strength from its irony and ambiguity. Thus he wrote in notes to his actors:

> There is evidence in the text that the play was written in a ferment of excitement. The author was quite unable to resist the attraction of a new idea or a new twist to the plot, even if this confused the unity of the whole: the result is a flamboyant and sensational piece which changes constantly – pungent, moralistic, melodramatic, comic, allegorical, violent, poetic, bawdy, tragic, absurd, ironic – the moods tumble over each other, blend and alternate in exuberant profusion. Each element is contrasted against the others: it is this equivocal interplay, expressed in perfectly matched coruscating verse which makes the play so surprising:[17]

It was this element of surprise which Shelton wished to keep alive throughout the performance by attacking the audience with the stark realities of the text transformed into physical action:

> One must be faithful to the author, and present the play which he wrote, but this does not necessarily mean adopting a quasi-reverential approach: indeed, I believe, that such a course would be disastrous ... The audience must be brow-beaten and carried along by the sheer attack of the playing ... there is a tremendous force and pace in the text – we must transfer it into physical action. The play is frankly sensational, and requires flamboyant and expansive acting, athletic acting. We

accept the physical presence of the audience as easily as does a music-hall comic – we play the show at them at point-blank range.[18]

Thus he envisaged the performance as being stylized rather than naturalistic. He recognized the play's debt not only to medieval drama but to renaissance mannerism, both of which allow for the presentation or depiction of a commentator standing aside from the action so as to note the moral content of the work. Thus on a multi-levelled set the text's inherent moral commentary was presented by the respective characters, Vindice or Hippolito stepping down towards the audience so as to instruct them on the meaning of the action. The unlocalized nature of the fuscous design created by Shelton and Dee Kelly enabled the production to move swiftly and alertly from one seemingly contradictory event to another without destroying the aesthetic pattern. The set of black with bare boards, white plaster, spikes and heavy studded central doors to the rear over which was a gallery, enabled him to introduce his characters either in shaded darkness or in the flamboyant colours of the decadent society. The central section of the stage was raised[19] allowing aisles at either side and steps down to the auditorium. Scaffolding from the aisles rising to the gallery completed the five or six levels in which his actors were to perform, with the addition of an entrance and exit tunnel behind the rear door in which figures were to lurk eavesdropping on the actions depicted. At all times the audience was reminded that this was a stage – the lighting apparatus for example, was clearly visible – on which a black farce was being enacted. Assiduous light picked out the characters exposing the degeneracy of their evil. Thus the audience's vision was allowed to wander in a controlled fashion over the entire area. In the 'bony lady' episode consequently, as the Duke lay dying on the central platform, Spurio and the Duchess entered on the gallery above to conduct their incestuous affair. Likewise in the opening scene the characters, having colourfully and flamboyantly paraded around and across the stage froze in pools of acid light, as Vindice, dark-cloaked, weaved his way among them to present his sombre chorus. Quite correctly Mr Shelton had recognized within this Jacobean tragedy elements of decadence, horror and black farce acutely appropriate to a twentieth-century audience that shared with its predecessor uncertainties about the role and purpose of mankind, its societies and institutions. The play, he felt, could stand on its own terms and was consequently presented without cuts or additions, the actors working from facsimiles of the early quarto. Not surprisingly the result was well-received by the press. The *Scotsman* (15 July 1965) and the *Glasgow Herald* (15 July 1965) agreed that, in correctly balancing tragedy with comedy, the production had achieved a sensitivity which fully justified its presentation and appropriateness for the modern theatre.

Trevor Nunn's famous RSC production which made its first appearance at Stratford in the following year, 1966, was in marked contrast to Shelton's. Nunn decided from the start that certain alterations would have to be made to the text in order to clarify it for the modern audience. The ambiguities appeared too great, the Christian morality too strong, and both consequently had to be reduced through heavy editing. John Barton was asked to produce a script which would convey the play's aims and purpose. His response was linear in that he attempted to emphasize the revenge motif in the presentation of the protagonist and to isolate evil by explaining some of the central ironies, rather than just hoping that they might be perceived in action. Thus Hippolito's moralistic soliloquy (III. v. 36–42) on the hypocrisy of respectability was replaced by one commenting on the motives, impetus and sensuousness of revenge:

> A witness: to what?   Why, to my brother's vengeance.
> What's that to me?   I like't, and I like it not.
> This vengeance is a law prompted by nature,
> Promulgate by our blood, which when we broach it
> Makes that blood thrill, as now my brother's doth
> Sure, 'tis a violent joy, and I suspect it:
> Nay, I must doubt myself, for mine own veins
> Joy, too, i'th' very moment of suspect.
> Why do they so? Alas, we dare not know:
> Most perilous actions, dire and dangerous,
> Are lesser danger than to search ourselves, –
> Masks off, that's fearful. Yet the masks being on,
> I fear the first fires of our outward flames
> Are fouler than our vices' outward names.[20]

Such a speech instructed the audience that the revengers

themselves were at heart evil and to be seen in that light throughout the play. It consequently polarized our response to the protagonist by reducing ambiguity in favour of interpretation. Thus having defined the ephemera of Vindice and Hippolito their extreme opposite had to be created in order to redress the moral balance. This was done by giving greater emphasis to the morality of Antonio at the expense of the protagonist. The order of the play was rearranged so as to bring Antonio's relation of the circumstances of his wife's death (I. iv.) closer to the beginning of the work. As it was Trevor Nunn opened the production with a masque depicting the rape of Antonio's wife. This was followed by Vindice's opening soliloquy and conversation with Hippolito. In 1966 the Gratiana-Castiza scene was then omitted – although re-introduced in the subsequent revivals – to be replaced by the Antonio scene. In all performances, however, the Antonio scene came at the end of Act I. Sc. i. before the trial of Junior Brother. Antonio thereby told his sad story not only to Hippolito but also to Vindice. This alteration provided Vindice with another motive for his deeds and through a newly written dialogue contrasted his evil with Antonio's Christian stoicism:

Antonio   His trial's appointed.
Vindice   Who shall judge him, think you?
Antonio   Grave men. Albeit the Duke must give the sentence.
Hippolito   He'll never doom him: what? – the Duchess' youngest son.
Antonio   Yet he'll be judged,
Vindice   But when?
Antonio   When heaven shall please.
Vindice   Deferr'd till doomsday? Nay, 'twill ne'er please me. Till we that love you may her vengers be.
Antonio   If you love me, or law, you'll hold your hand.
Vindice   Nay, Sir –
Antonio   Nay, nay, Sir. That must not be scanned: There are two laws, the Duke's and God's above. Learn this a little ere you talk of love.
Hippolito   And yet 'twere pity.

Similarly in the complex episode where Lussurioso goes in search of Spurio to kill him, whilst Spurio had gone in search of Lussurioso for the same purpose (II. iii.) a scene was introduced to explain the comic irony of the situation. As Lussurioso left for the Duchess's chamber Spurio returned from his abortive attempt at murder, cursing his servants for deluding him:

> *Spurio* He was not there! You are all villains, fablers!
> *1st Servant* O good my Lord.
> *Spurio* Lussurioso was not there!
> *2nd Servant* 'Twas his intent to meet there.
> *Spurio* Not there, not there! I wonder where he went?
> *3rd Servant* Wher'er I doubt not he was foully bent.
> *Spurio* Go find him villains, and report him right:
> 'Tis certain he's at foulness now 'tis night.[21]

To explain irony in such a manner is to some extent to negate it, but this was necessary if the rapidity of the narrative was to be maintained. Similarly therefore the Dondolo episode (II. i. 10–24) and Junior Brother's execution scene (III. iv.) were omitted, as being extraneous to the linear development of the play as a whole. Consequently the complex juxtapositioning of Tourneur's original pattern was smoothed away as being no longer viable. Such a decision may have meant a certain loss of theatrical effect. To avoid this Trevor Nunn introduced specific locations for his action – a church for the opening scenes, a throne room, a bedroom, a sewing room with dummies for the Gratiana-Castiza scene, a gymnasium, a lodge or vault, and a torture chamber – and within these presented specific events. Thus a fencing routine opened I. iii., whilst II. ii., saw Lussurioso manipulated by a masseur. Act IV. Scene i. was conducted to the background of torture, a man hung on a rack at the rear of the stage whilst Lussurioso at one point took the hand of a lady-in-waiting, forcing her to press a lever causing the screaming victim more pain. Surprise tactics were also employed. Lussurioso, for example, assaulting the Duke and Duchess (II. iii.) in his attempt to kill Spurio, forced a hideously bald mother from the bed, whilst later in a newly written scene following v. i. 167, he spat at her as he pronounced her banishment. The rest of the court laughed. The affinity of the play to the dance of death was also exploited. The final masque scenes were presented with the characters wearing skull-vizards. Likewise Spurio and the Duchess, watched by the dying Duke, danced to their incestuous bed. Here Mr Barton, employing material from *The Atheist's Tragedy*, rewrote the episode so as to expose the vulgarity of their incest through sexual innuendo:

> Music: a Dance by Torchlight[22]
> *Spurio*   Like you the music?
> *Duchess*. Ay, and long to dance.
> *Spurio*   Shall's do't by torchlight?
> *Duchess*   Yes.
> *Spurio*   Or in the dark?
> *Duchess*   Fie, an your torch be out our dance is done:
>   I mean to dance till morning by the maypole.
> *Spurio*   In the English manner, then?
> *Duchess*   Or in the French.
> *Spurio*   Fie, they dance backward.
> *Duchess*   So; let's try out countries.
>   And learn new ways to climb.
> *Spurio*   Ay, to the mountain,
> *Duchess*   There's many ways.... (III. v.)

Thus a complex theatrical event was achieved by the director which was enhanced by the professionalism of his actors. Ian Richardson's Vindice dominated the whole spitting out his bitter hatred in the 1966 performance although toning down the vehemence for a mellower presentation in the subsequent revivals. Alan Howard's Lussurioso was shockingly degenerate demonstrating 'a limpid sensuality which occasionally freezes into a disgusting awkwardness – the statuary of lust'.[23] Brenda Bruce as the Duchess,[24] Norman Rodway as the Bastard and David Waller, to be succeeded by the thinner, colder Nicholas Selby, as the Duke, all gave a hideous clarity to the picture presented, and when in 1969 Helen Mirren joined the cast, a dimension of repressed sensuality was given to the role of Castiza.

The production received mixed notices from the press. Some critics such as Harold Hobson (*The Sunday Times* 9 October 1966) showed a concern about the advisability and appropriateness of the play for presentation. Was the RSC becoming too obsessed with the theatre of cruelty? Others such as *The Times* special correspondent (6 October 1966) praised John Barton's adaptation as making sense of a rather confused original text. Yet B.A. Young (*Financial Times* 6 October 1966) objected that the director had 'surrendered to his difficulties and played the hard parts for laughs.' Hilary Spurling, in contrast (*The Spectator* 14 October 1966) thought the company took itself too seriously and naturalistically, employing an acting style 'perfected' for Shakespeare to present a dramatist of a different order. Ronald Bryden (*Observer* 9 October 1966) felt that a correct balance had been achieved between 'terror and absurdity' and that the production was a landmark in a movement away from naturalism, towards something more appropriate to the modern stage. Hilary Spurling showed concern over Christopher Morley's sombre black and steel grey costumes, feeling that the work demanded gaudy colours whereas Eric Shorter (*Daily Telegraph* 6 October 1966) thought the 'ink-black setting' brought a truthfulness to the work's 'deadly decadence'. In the following year some critics such as Don Chapman (*Oxford Mail* 5 May 1967) felt that familiarity reduced the impact of surprise which some scenes, such as the exposure of the Duchess's baldness, had added to the play. Gareth Lloyd Evans however in a major article (*Stratford-upon-Avon Herald* 12 May 1967) rightly praised the company for exploiting the truly satiric quality of the work with directorial vision and accomplished acting. By the time the production reached London in 1969 it was generally accepted as being of major significance although the controversies continued as to the artistic and aesthetic balances that were or were not maintained.[25]

Difficult in its text, controversial but successful in its RSC performance, and yet vital in the truth to its original design at Pitlochry, *The Revenger's Tragedy* creates its own ambience of the sterility of evil and simultaneously comments on its self-imposed decadence. It is only within this complex relationship of the two that its 'metaphysical core' can be found. At once it instructs and illustrates, and as we view it in the totality of its artistic image, it presents to us, both in text and production, an intrinsic dramatic pattern; an aesthetic artifact just as appropriate to the twentieth-century as it was to Jacobean London.

4 Volpone

Reviewing the Peter Hall–Paul Scofield *Volpone* at the National Theatre in 1977 John Barber commented:

> What I missed was the manic Jonsonian tension, the massive voltage in man's bitter trouncing of human greed and pettiness. Perhaps the thing looked too pretty. Perhaps the laughter was too good-tempered, the sensuality too polite, Scofield himself too noble a figure. Or perhaps the director is too amiable a man. (*Daily Telegraph* 27 April 1977)

Volpone is not an amiable play. It is vicious in its humour and savage in its portrayal of human values and thus, although it was given an entertaining production by Peter Hall, it could not be expressed in a performance that steered clear of its acute cynicism.

Modern appreciation stressing the serious undertones of this comedy can be said to have begun with L.C. Knight's evaluation that it helped to expose Jonson's anti-acquisitive attitude by focusing upon the twin evils of lust and greed.[1] This insight has subsequently been developed by John J. Enck into an appreciation of the appropriateness of the work for the twentieth-century,[2] and an understanding by Alvin Kernan and George Hibbard among others that the metaphor through which the evils are explored, evaluated and eventually enveloped is one of deceit and role play.[3] Consequently deception of the self as well as of others can now be seen as the dominant theme. The result is that director or actor facing the prospect of performance has the difficult task of finding an approach which will adequately expose the complex intermingling of greed, lust, decadence, degeneracy, perjury and moral disease through a structural facade designed to amuse. The play's success depends on a tension being continually maintained within the reaction of the audience between laughter and the acknowledgement of its barbarous cause. One way forward is to take the work in stages that build up the final image, realizing that at each moment only one aspect of the complex whole is being developed and that in the end all must be fitted together like an aesthetic jig-saw puzzle.

A basic premise of the play is that acquisitiveness has the effect of reducing characters to a form of bestiality. There is no spiritual dimension since the soul has been changed by a diseased alchemy into a glister of gold. Consequently we are presented with a world of reversed moral values. Man is illustrated as employing rationality in a manner in which animals use instinct. His reason is debased in its perverted relationship to the animalistic. Jonas Barish has instructively written:

> It is unnatural for baboons and apes and parrots to counterfeit human behaviour. It is equally unnatural for men to imitate beasts. It argues a perversion of their essential humanity. It is not for nothing, then, that the chief characters of the play fit into one zoological classification or another. As men, they duplicate the habits of beasts; as beasts, they brutishly travesty humanity. They belong to the genus *monster* – half man, half brute – that order of fabulous creatures whose common denominator is their unnaturalness, their lack of adherence to whatever category of being nature has assigned them.[4]

The grotesque horror of Volpone's creatures, therefore, is not that suddenly like Kafka's Gregor[5] they awake as beasts but that they are continually in the act of an attempted metamorphosis: that they employ their rationality to reduce their humanity. Thus a paradox of the play is that reason is continually employed to destroy itself.

To understand how this occurs in its simplest manner we can turn first to the sub-plot and in particular to Sir Politic Would-Be's attempt to disguise himself as a tortoise. The action is an escape from the reality of his human condition. Aspiring always to be something that he is not Sir Politic illustrates the absurdity of his pretensions by crawling into the skin or shell of another animal in the cause of self preservation. Beneath all the humour there is something rather pathetic and grotesque in the action since it symbolises a reduction of his humanity and finally exposes the perversity of his existence. Jonson presents a caricature of the English traveller – the self-opinionated and supposedly refined English knight – finally and unmercifully to debase him in a scene of uncompromising ridicule:

> *1st Merchant* St. Mark! What beast is this?
> *Peregrine* It is a fish.
> *2nd Merchant* Come out here.
> *Peregrine* Nay, you may strike him, sir, and tread upon him – He'll bear a cart.
> *1st Merchant* What, to run over him?
> *Peregrine* Yes.
> *3rd Merchant* Let's jump upon him.
> *2nd Merchant* Can he not go?
> *Peregrine* He creeps, sir.
> *1st Merchant* Let's see him creep. *[Prods him with sword.]*
> *Peregrine* No, good sir, you will hurt him.
> *2nd Merchant* Heart, I'll see him creep, or prick his guts.
> *3rd Merchant* Come out here.
> *Peregrine [Aside to Sir Politic]* Pray you sir, creep a little.
> *1st Merchant* Forth.
> *2nd Merchant* Yet further.
> *Peregrine [To Sir Politic]* Good sir. Creep.
> *2nd Merchant* We'll see his legs.
> *[They pull off the shell and discover him.]* (v. iv. 64–72)[6]

This cruel exposure is the logical, comic climax of Sir Politic's portrayal throughout but beneath the laughter remains the unsightly vision of the lengths to which insignificant man will go in order to justify his self regard, indulgence or aggrandisement. Creeping on his belly in total submission to men stamping on his bestial shell this fop provides as vivid a portrayal of degradation as the perverted role-play indulged in by the man playing the Judge in Jean Genet's *The Balcony*:

> *The Judge* ... it's all right to be mean and make me yearn,

> even prance, make me dance, drool, sweat, whinny with impatience, crawl ... do you want me to crawl?
> *The Executioner [to the Judge]* Crawl.
> *The Judge* I'm proud!
> *The Executioner [threateningly]* Crawl!
> *[The Judge, who was on his knees, lies flat on his stomach and crawls slowly towards the Thief. As he crawls forward, the Thief moves back.]*
> *The Executioner* Good. Continue.
> *The Judge [to the Thief]* You're quite right, you rascal, to make me crawl after my judgeship, but if you were to refuse for good, you hussy, it would be criminal ...
> *The Thief [haughtily]* Call me Madame, and ask politely.
> *The Judge* Will I get what I want?
> *The Thief [coyly]* It costs a lot – stealing does.
> *The Judge* I'll pay! ... Madame! Madame, please, I beg of you. I'm willing to lick your shoes, but tell me you're a thief ...
> *The Thief [in a cry]* Not yet! Lick! Lick! Lick first![7]

To satisfy his masochistic indulgence in his role Genet's brothel house character suffers the indignities of total submission, wriggling on the floor as an animal. Sir Politic's portrayal does not contain the same sensuality but is seen with a detachment in Jonson's satiric stance.[8] Nevertheless the two postures equate as do the essential themes concerning the state in which civilized man may appear. To some extent Jonson's dramatic technique here and in the play as a whole looks forward to Genet's creation of 'anti-worlds'. In plays such as *Deathwatch* or *The Maids* the modern dramatist creates societies so alien to a normal moral environment that in their negative portrayal they create their own standards of behaviour. A morality and gradation of evil exists in the prison world of *Deathwatch*, where Lefranc desperately attempts to be accepted as a member of the caged society, by the murderer Green Eyes. In *The Maids* and later plays such as *The Balcony* or *The Blacks* these negative environments creating their own positivism find their expression in role-play and mask. Acting becomes the photographic negative of the real world to such an extent that in *The Maids* the servants Solange and Claire continually acting out how they will kill their mistress, agree to Claire, in the role of Madame, actually drinking poison:

Claire I say: my tea.
Solange But, Madame.
Claire Good. Continue.
Solange But, Madame, it's cold.
Claire I'll drink it anyway. Let me have it. *[Solange brings the tray]* And you've poured it into the best, the finest tea set. *[She takes the cup and drinks ...]*[9]

Only the finest china merits Claire's macabre drama. Her roleplay kills her although in her death she sees the positive fulfillment of the act that she has played throughout. It is in this respect that the *Volpone* world is not totally dissimilar to that created by the modern dramatist. Sir Politic Would-Be is not the only character wallowing in pretence. He is just one reflection of a society dedicated to the maintenance of disguise and the distortion of normal moral principles; Volpone as fox; Mosca as fly; Corvino, crow; Corbaccio, raven; Voltore, vulture. In this respect they present a hideous sight of greed in their attempted translation to their equivalent beast gathering for carrion wealth. Thus Mosca, the fat fly, is instructed to suck their blood as they hear of Volpone's death:

Mosca Hark,
   There's some already.
Volpone   Look.
Mosca   It is the vulture;
   He has the quickest scent.
Volpone   I'll to my place,
   Thou, to thy posture. *[Concealing himself]*
Mosca I am set
Volpone   But Mosca,
   Play the artificer now, torture 'em rarely. (v. ii. 107–11)

All acting as animals a position is created where each tries to prey on the other developing a situation where everything is achieved through the constant affirmation that the truth is a lie and the lie, truth. The result is that health is disease; purity, folly; spirituality, gold, and life, death. The normal touchstones of reality disappear so that even when Volpone is thought to be dead he is alive. Jonson's reversed order of existence is here not far from Genet's theatre since a mirror image[10] of society is being established: everything taken for granted as normal by the characters themselves is, in the actual world of the audience, left to right or right to left. Some prisoners do look on their crimes as a profession, to which others aspire but are found wanting. Servants do hate masters to an extent of self-destruction, not only in the manner of Solange and Claire but of Iago and Vindice. The civilized role-play of society where men dress as judges, soldiers, priests or academics, disguises inner aspirations, ambitions and desires which may or may not be honourable to society at large. What crime then is Volpone committing? –

>   ... I gain
> No common way: I use no trade, no venture;
> I wound no earth with ploughshares; fat no beasts
> To feed the shambles; have no mills for iron,
> Oil, corn, or men, to grind 'em into powder;
> I blow no subtle glass; expose no ships
> To threat'nings of the furrrow-facèd sea;
> I turn no moneys in the public bank;
> Nor usure private... (I. i. 32–40)

To this protagonist on a Venetian stage ruled by wealth, trade and exploitation a form of inverted prostitution[11] seems to be exactly what his clients desire. They will invest their money in the rotting flesh of age to sample the delights of their cunning in the expectation of plenty:

> *Voltore* But, Mosca –
> *Mosca*   Age will conquer.
> *Voltore*   Pray thee hear me.
>   Am I inscribed his heir for certain?
>   ... am I sole heir?
> *Mosca*   Without partner sir... (I. iii. 32–3, 44–5)

Just as they will listen to a notorious mountebank falsely expounding on the value of his restorative liquor:

> O, health! health! the blessing of the rich! the riches of the poor! who can buy thee at too dear a rate, since there is no

enjoying this world without thee? Be not then so sparing of your purses, honourable gentlemen, as to abridge the natural course of life... (II. ii. 84–8)

Volpone's role-play as invalid or doctor is consequently emblematic of the society in which it operates as a whole. As L.C. Knights noted and as has been constantly re-iterated, even the avocatori judging the complexities of deceit 'display a new-found politeness to Mosca when it seems that he is heir.'[12] Money in itself is part of the disguise indulged in by the society and signified for example by Mosca donning Volpone's 'habit of clarissimo' (v. iii. 103). Simultaneously through a complex set of mirror images the dramatist here presents the reflections of a sham world based solely on material values. Thus the self-reflecting portraits of the society assume the deformities of an incestuous union in the presence of eunuch, dwarf and hermaphrodite, a symbolic trinity of the grotesque progeny not merely of Volpone's mind but of the civilization to which he belongs. They perform before him a satiric interlude on the normality of civilized thought. Thus they parody Neo-Platonic ideals of the relationship of beauty and truth, as partially realized in Pythagorian concepts of harmony, through deliberately exaggerating and distorting the more controversial elements of the philosopher's thought:

Nano For know *[Pointing to Androgyno]*, here is enclosed the soul of Pythagoras,
That juggler divine, as hereafter shall follow;
Which soul (fast and loose, sir) came first from Apollo
And was breathed into Aethalides, Mercurius his son,
Where it had the gift to remember all that ever was done.
(I. ii. 6–10)[13]

Twisted in mind and body, seeing only weakness in the philosophy of Western civilization Nano, Castrone and Androgyno are the ultimate reflection of Volpone's degenerate universe. Appropriately they first display their decadence in a play within a play and fittingly it is the dwarf and eunuch who are entrusted finally to bring all to a close by reporting Volpone's 'death'. So infatuated by his part Volpone is allowed like Solange and Claire, to lose himself within it and thereby ironically to become inseparably fused with the role he has enacted:

> ...our judgment on thee
> Is, that thy substance all be straight confiscate
> To the hospital of the *Incurabili*;
> And, since the most was gotten by imposture,
> By feigning lame, gout, palsy and such diseases,
> Thou art to lie in prison, cramped with irons,
> Till thou be'st sick and lame indeed ... (v. xii. 118–24)[14]

The difference however between Volpone and Claire lies in the attitude of the respective dramatists. Both are writing in a capitalist age of materialism but, whereas Genet has abandoned all thoughts of spiritual significance, Jonson retains a basis in the positive morality of his own and, he hopes, the audience's Christian values.[15] In Genet therefore the mirrors are never taken away but are rather continually increased in their density taking characters and audience alike into the experience of the unconquerable and incomprehensible maze that is the absurdity of action, society and life itself. As Claire dies Solange paradoxically talks of the living death of Madame:

> The orchestra is playing brilliantly. The attendant is raising the red velvet curtain. He bows. Madame is descending the stairs. Her furs brush against the green plants. Madame steps into the car. Monsieur is whispering sweet nothings in her ear. She would like to smile, but she is dead. She rings the bell. The porter yawns. He opens the door. Madame goes up the stairs. She enters her flat – but, Madame is dead. Her two maids are alive: they've just risen up, free, from Madame's icy form. All the maids were present at her side – not they themselves, but rather the hellish agony of their names. And all that remains of them to float about Madame's airy corpse is the delicate perfume of the holy maidens which they were in secret. We are beautiful, joyous, drunk, and free! (pp. 42–3)

All is illusion. Life, death, freedom and joy in a drugged performance of both existence and non-existence: an ephemeral, abstract, absurd event. This however is not so with Jonson. Even though the avocatori implicate themselves in the role-play Jonson refuses to allow the illusion to continue beyond the drama. Volpone overacts his part, losing himself in his fantasy. His judgement mimics his performance and forces him back to the crude reality of life under the heavens, away from his stage, 'This is called mortifying of a fox' (v. xii. 125)[16]. Volpone's statement is one affirming the existence of a positive life, one which belongs to the audience itself, that is to the society creating the play. As has often been illustrated[17] at the end of the performance the actor playing the great artificer comes forward to deliver the epilogue:

The seasoning of a play is the applause.
Now, though Fox be punished by the laws,
He yet doth hope there is no suffering due
For any fact which he hath done 'gainst you.
If there be, censure him – here he doubtful stands.
If not, fare jovially, and clap your hands. (v. xii. 152–7)

Beneath all the disguise is a man like the author who belongs to the real world of the audience wishing for approbation and applause.[18]

This realization of the affinity and yet difference between the worlds of the performance and that of the audience is not completely left to the final scene. Throughout the drama Jonson has cleverly balanced satiric caricature with dramatic illusion to produce what we might now term as an important alienation effect. As seen, Sir Politic's exaggerated portrayal prevents an emotional empathy being established during the tortoise episode. Similarly Lady Politic's interruptions of Volpone's sports (III. iv.) help to distance the audience so as to prepare an intellectual foundation for the ensuing emotionally vivid scene with Celia (III. vii.). One of the results of the technique is that through the Celia episode the dramatist is able to define the degeneracy into which society has fallen. First, locked up as an animal by a man in the situation of self-imposed metamorphosis, the wife is then prostituted for the sake of her husband's commercial gain. When she attempts to refuse, Corvino demonstrates the full perversity of his hideous imagination:

Celia Sir, kill me, rather. I will take poison,
   Eat burning coals, do anything –
Corvino   Be damned!

> Heart, I will drag thee hence, home, by the hair;
> Cry thee a strumpet through the streets; rip up
> Thy mouth, unto thine ears; and slit thy nose,
> Like a raw rochet – Do not tempt me, come.
> Yield, I am loath – Death, I will buy some slave,
> Whom I will kill, and bind thee to him, alive;
> And at my window, hang you forth – devising
> Some monstrous crime, which I, in capital letters,
> Will eat into thy flesh, with acquafortis
> And burning corsives, on this stubborn breast.
> Now, by the blood thou hast incensed, I'll do'it.
> *Celia* Sir, what you please, you may; I am your martyr.
> (III. vii. 94–107)

Celia's cries here need not be taken as a portrayal of a moral alternative to Corvino's illusion since, unlike Tourneur's Castiza, neither she nor Bonario are emphasized enough to provide such a purpose.[19] Rather they may be seen as poignant comments on her vulnerability illustrating the absence of moral stability in Corvino's society. Simultaneously however her presence in the play does illustrate how close the real and the fictitious worlds are to each other. The wife is supposed to be subject even as a 'martyr' to the husband. Yet he first imprisoning her will only grant a release so as to bind her to decaying flesh, the feigned impotency of Volpone. As a character on stage Celia can find no foundations in this nightmare of debauchery. She can only cry to something beyond the dream:

> O God, and his good angels! wither, wither
> Is shame fled human breasts? that with such ease
> Men dare put off your honours, and their own?
> Is that, which ever was the cause of life,
> Now placed beneath the basest circumstance?
> And modesty an exile made, for money? (III. vii. 133–8)

Though this speech is addressed to God Jonson is here employing Celia as a chorus, commenting through her on the world he presents. The timing of the statement is precise since worse actions are to ensue testifying to its accuracy. Neither honour nor modesty exist in Volpone's world as disease rises from its bed to add its awful spectre to her nightmare. Purulent masculinity descends on its victim disguising its sepsis in the ironies, not of Genet's fine china, but of poetry:

>   Why droops my Celia?
> Thou hast in place of a base husband found
> A worthy lover; use thy fortune well,
> With secrecy, and pleasure. See, behold,
> What thou art queen of; not in expectation,
> As I feed others, but possessed, and crowned.
> See, here, a rope of pearl, and each more orient
> Than that brave Egyptian queen caroused;
> Dissolve, and drink 'em. See, a carbuncle,
> May put out both the eyes of our St Mark;
> A diamond, would have bought Lollia Paulina,
> When she came in like star-light, hid with jewels
> That were the spoils of provinces; take these,
> And wear, and lose 'em; yet remains an ear-ring
> To purchase them again, and this whole state.
>   (III. vii. 185–99)

Uttering these words Scofield's Volpone, as one reviewer noted, committed an 'aesthetic rape' (Robert Cushman, *Observer*, 1 May 1977) but the actor himself lacked the physical repulsion which should accompany the hypocrisy of the language. Visually Scofield was too handsome for the part. Volpone must be an oily creature, repugnant in appearance, so as to expose the contrast between the beauty of his words and the grotesque horror of his design.[20] Such an incongruity will then in turn emphasize the symbols of moral degeneracy being employed: pearls, diamonds, jewels. This luxurious vision is one of an insatiate lust for flesh, wealth and their attendant pleasures:

> The heads of parrots, tongues of nightingales,
> The brains of peacocks, and of ostriches
> Shall be our food; and, could we get the phoenix,
> Though nature lost her kind, she were our dish.
>   (III. vii. 202–5)

It is the fictitious world of chimeras and dreams, a world belonging to acts and role-play, a world close enough to be recognized as a reflective image of society and yet distant enough to allow an instinctive condemnation of its progress whilst we simultaneously appreciate its humour and ingenuity. It is here that the play's complex set of balances between the comic and the grotesque, the fictitious and the real, the structure and the theme are held perfectly steady.

It is therefore the relationship not only between the characters and illusions in the play but between the action of the stage and the receptive presence of the audience that should produce the total artistic effect of *Volpone*. An immediate problem for the modern theatre must consequently lie in Jonson's faith in traditional Christian values since this is not necessarily shared by the majority of twentieth-century spectators. Nevertheless as stated in connection with *Dr Faustus*, whether Christian in belief or not Western audiences have a cultural basis founded on Christianity from which they cannot escape. Jonson's balances may still work since the majority of secular elements in society still adhere to moral codes that find an origin in the Christian tradition. Thus although parallels can be drawn to illustrate the affinity of Jonson's dramatic vision with those of modern dramatists such as Genet helping to bridge a four-hundred-year interlude, the play in the end has to stand on its own terms. In an age acquainted with Kafka's *Metamorphosis* or Ionesco's *Rhinoceros* there must be a danger of going too far in the emphasis of the bestial transformations in the play. Tyrone Guthrie's productions of 1964 and 1968 presented Jonson's characters as the animals they portrayed even to the extent of providing the birds with six-inch beaks. The performers actually studied the mannerisms of their appropriate beasts and portrayed themselves as such on stage. There was too much movement, too many twitches and although the performances were amazingly clever they lacked the poignant subtlety of the original design as E.B. Partridge in 1958 had prophesied that they would:

> If a literal identification were made, if, that is, Voltore were called Mr Vulture and appeared in the guise of a large black bird, the effect might be comic fantasy and even satire, but it would lack the vigour and the scorn that Jonson achieves by having an advocate compared to a vulture. Probably Voltore was dressed to suggest a vulture ... but he would always have been seen as a man.[21]

An earlier post war production at the Shakespeare Memorial Theatre, however found problems in timidity rather than aggression. Sir Ralph Richardson was criticized as being too restrained in the part of Volpone, the drama critic of *The Times* (16 July 1952) commenting on the lack of the terror that should accompany our laughter as we watch the conduct of the evil mind. This production by George Devine was lavish in its stage effects almost operatically turning the scene from Volpone's luxurious bed to the glories of the Venetian landscape, complete with the grand canal and its accompanying gondolas. Irving Wardle recalls:

> For this production, Devine mobilized the long neglected machinery installed during the Bridges-Adams régime. This included a sliding stage split in the middle with a 22-foot wing clearance on each side. Under the sliding stage were two massive lifts which between them could fill the entire space left vacant by the sliding stage. Additionally there were two revolves in the Prompt and O.P. corners. Devine used the lot. Volpone's bed-chamber with its vast four-poster slid out of view to make room for the arrival of the Senate, arising from the deep like a mighty Venetian Wurlitzer. Houses stood or spun round in the corners. The sets were by Malcolm Pride who framed them within a Venetian surround complete with gondolas ... Inevitably there came the night of a power failure, but the stage management were equal to that. They took up the curtain and gave the audience the added spectacle of the stage staff cranking sets into position with huge windlasses.[22]

On less eventful nights the emphasis on the staging was much admired by some reviewers although *Punch* (30 July 1952) saw it as a distraction from the imaginative poetry on which so much of the play depends. The most significant aspect of the production about which all reviewers agreed, was Anthony Quayle's portrayal of an oily, repulsive, mincing Mosca.

The two major English productions in the 1970s to some extent refined both the approaches made by Devine and Guthrie. Richard David's 1972 production at the Bristol Old Vic continued to emphasize the bestial element of the work although he withdrew from the extravagances of the Guthrie vision. The strength of David's concept as Brian Parker notes was more in the *mise-en-scène* than in the costume and manners of the characters:

> The constructivist set was basically three tall, spindly platforms, with the one at stage left towering as high as twenty feet up into the flies. The birds' entrances to Volpone's bedroom were made by swooping down from this height along intersecting diagonal ramps, which not only established the image of circling predators but also allowed some interesting overlappings of scenes, of the kind suggested by Jonson's own use of 'One knocks without,' to indicate new arrivals before the previous scene has finished. Other bestiary features were a large, round, burrowlike opening over the middle platform and a down-stage trap into which Bonario and Celia were thrust into prison. In the scene where Corvino interrupts 'Scoto's' wooing of Celia, Mosca slid into this trap head foremost like a fly into a sewer, while the crow harried Volpone up the ramps and into the burrow. The whole set was painted a curious greenish-gold with lumpy encrustations, simultaneously suggesting ordure and decaying wealth, and it was appropriately dominated by a large hanging image of the Lion of St. Mark.[23]

Peter Hall's production with a set by John Bury was in marked contrast to that of David and Guthrie. A classical Venice was to dominate although not in the heavy manner of Devine but rather designed to aid the rapidity of the action. Three ceramic tiled 'avenues radiated off into the blackness through pointed iron archways'[24] and folding doors that allowed a 'change from beaten gold to bureaucratic white and a skeletal frame adumbrating the shape of St. Mark's.'[25] Yet as Michael Billington noted the whole gave a distracting impression that it was too 'cool and precise for the tumultuous Jonsonian world'. Perhaps the definitive production of the play, if there can ever be one, must lie somewhere between these two approaches in its complex yet crucial attempt to balance correctly the humour and the horror which are the play's essence and life.

5 Measure for Measure

In the theatre no less than in the study Shakespeare's *Measure for Measure* proves to be a difficult play. Its central character, the Duke, is inconsistent in characterization whilst its theme on the measure of justice is handled with a structural artificiality which jars both on stage and page. Yet paradoxically the play seems to be immensely popular with directors, actors and audiences and has received numerous productions on the post-war British stage, with the 1970s in particular being a fruitful period for it.

In attempts to extricate the play from its problems some critics have suggested that difficulties arise because evaluations tend to focus first on character rather than on plot.[1] John Barton, however, who mounted the play for the RSC in 1970 found such an idea in itself problematic. He stated in a later interview on the direction of the problem plays:

> When a director explores a play he is bound, primarily, to be doing so in terms of character and psychology, even though he may – indeed must – remind the actors that this is not necessarily what Shakespeare always demands of them. The exploration of character is not the only objective of rehearsals, but it is at the heart of the acting tradition in England, and one has to work within that tradition.[2]

At the heart of his *Measure for Measure* was the Duke who Wilson Knight in 1930 had seen in Angelo's words as 'a power divine', the controlling lord.[3] Barton's production reacted strongly against this concept. The Duke might be central but he was no God. Thus Anne Barton wrote in the programme:

> As for the Duke; if he is, as some critics maintain, an image of Providence, there would seem to be chaos in Heaven. His attempt to stage-manage a human reality far too complex for

such arbitary ordering is inefficient. It also reveals his inability to understand the thoughts and feelings of other people.[4]

Consequently Sebastian Shaw was cast as an old fumbling Duke wearing spectacles and a Holbein cap. He smiled his way through the action that he had perpetrated in a manner denoting a man lacking in both confidence and control. His grin, his looks of concern, were a disguise for the impotency of power which he admits in the text:

> Sith 'twas my fault to give the people scope,
> 'Twould be my tyranny to strike and gall them
> For what I bid them do ... (I. iii. 35–7)[5]

These weaknesses in the Duke were central to the production. Rather than facing up to his own deficiencies the impotent ruler abrogated power to a cold Puritan. The text is again explicit:

> Therefore indeed, my father,
> I have on Angelo impos'd the office;
> Who may in th'ambush of my name, strike home
> An yet my nature never in the fight
> To do in slander... (I. iii. 39–43)

Sebastian Shaw's Duke consequently gave the dirty job to Angelo whilst he, disguised as a friar, hesitated, interfered or just hovered around the court supporting a Cheshire grin. This old man could neither exercise nor relinquish power but was rather a portrait of ineffectuality. He constantly changed his role to suit the immediacy of the situation so that the smile might move into a temporary frown of disgust or irritation, but in totality he remained a vision, the grin after the cat had disappeared. In the final scene as he pushed through supernumeraries to make his proposal to Isabella he met a wall of silence. His ineffectuality was still with him. Embarrassed as ever he fumbled with his spectacles and looked sad yet falsely-stoical in his role-play. This interpretation, though not appreciated by all reviewers, allowed the production a direction whereby the complexities of the action had a sub-textual cause in the constant presence of weakness. An impotency in the portrayal of the Duke influenced and corresponded to Angelo's and Isabella's forms of extremism. The movement from ineffectuality to tyranny, corruption and hypocrisy proved logical and comprehensible.

Although thematically pertinent John Barton's production however proved intellectually cold for what Stuart Burge displayed to be a highly comic play in his 1976 Birmingham Repertory Company production at the Edinburgh Festival. He moved away from psychological or moral interpretations of the drama by allowing the centrality of his Duke, Bernard Lloyd, to emphasize the work's inherent comedy. This was a young Duke's masquerade in which no-one would be hurt, and the audience would be entertained with the frivolity of the action. Thus the Duke first appeared with his face half-covered in foam as he was being rapidly shaved for his journey. He could not wait to be away in order to embark on his tricks and once in the friar's habit he gleefully rubbed his hands and began through winks, nods and direct address, to establish a comic rapport with the audience. There was nothing sinister here. All would be well, not from the point of view that the Duke had divine omnipotence but rather from the fact that he was the master of comic ceremonies reassuring the spectators throughout by his humour. We laughed with him at the follies of man, whilst intimations of his weakness or cruelty were swept aside in the rapidity of the action and entertainment. It was a grand, enjoyable festive event uncluttered with problems but lacking in thematic cohesion and strength.

A similar difficulty was apparent in the 1979 BBC production for the complete Shakespeare series. Sympathetically attractive Kenneth Colley's Duke comforted the worried, distraught Isabella, Kate Nelligan, with a fraternal arm. He became genuinely surprised, perplexed and unhappy when no repeal came for Claudio but his presentation necessarily jarred when later he lied in telling her of her brother's 'death'. (IV. iii. 106f.) Although this scene was well handled outside the prison, with John McEnery helping to distract attention from the difficulties by giving Lucio the appearance of a frustrated attraction towards the departing sister (IV. iii. 150–7), consistency in the Duke's characterization was still undermined. The remainder of the production appeared highly artificial in comparison with the first half of the play. The final scenes consequently appeared superfluous to the preceding action.

In 1979 two productions of the play were also presented in

London. Whereas in Peter Gill's production at the Riverside Studios George Baker played the Duke as 'an understanding family solicitor' (Milton Shulman, *Evening Standard*, 24 May 1979) Michael Pennington presented a more interesting character for Barry Kyle's RSC production at the Aldwych. Kyle's *Measure for Measure* began life in 1978 at Stratford, toured to Newcastle and, significantly re-cast, came to the Aldwych in November, 1979. Pennington, however, played the Duke at all three venues giving a performance in stark contrast to that of Sebastian Shaw in 1970. The RSC Duke had developed into someone who in the opening scene showed great agitation about the events he was to set in motion but who, once the role of friar had been assumed, became flirtatious with the intrigues and swift changes of fortune. This meant that though there was a danger of fragmentation in his portrayal there was also a real attempt at finding a balance between an understanding of the moral situation and a comic exploitation of the Duke's antics. Consequently one reviewer could correctly describe the Duke as 'eloquently world-weary' (*Sunday Telegraph*, 11 November 1979) whilst another could rightly see the same portrayal as 'an extremely brainy study of a one-time ascetic who, by putting on religious gear, discovers the worldliness buried inside his own nature' (Michael Billington, *Guardian*, 7 November 1979). As the play progressed Pennington's Duke was able to develop in an understanding of his own identity until for example, dressed as friar he could comically take a sly sip of Mariana's wine to refresh himself after so much intrigue and planning, or walk downstage to discuss the problems of authority, directly with the audience. A rapport between the Duke and the auditorium gradually developed strangely allowing both the character and the spectator to grow in the confidence of his ability to extricate some kind of order from the moral chaos. We were no longer in the presence of an impotent Duke or a lightly amusing one. It was rather a portrayal which as 'a model of how to play across the line of the text' (Robert Cushman, *Observer*, 11 November 1979) attempted the fusion of introspection and comic communication, conscience and intrigue. It consequently attempted to hold the complexities of the play together whilst allowing both the humour and the moral concerns to make themselves felt. Whether this was entirely successful or not and some reviewers more particularly in 1978 than 1979 had serious doubts,[6] it was an attempt at a more complex understanding of his character than had been hitherto explored.

More radical approaches to the Duke, however, had been attempted earlier in the decade. Barrie Ingham's Duke for Keith Hack's 1974 RSC production was presented as the grand sexual manipulator and designer of the whole action. Hack, influenced by Edward Bond, saw a sexual basis to the political hypocrises of the Viennese state.[7] Thus the Duke was a lecher fondling Isabella whilst pretending to comfort her, lustfully encompassing her in the folds of his cloak. The sexuality of this Duke was more perverse than that of Angelo, Lucio's words being taken at face value, 'He had some feeling for the sport; he knew the service...' (III. ii. 110–17). In one sense Hack went too far by over-interpreting the nuances of the play whilst in another not far enough in that he did not expand his ideas out of the text and into a new creation of his own making. It was this that Charles Marowitz did in 1975 at The Open Space.

In his version Marowitz employed creativity deliberately to highlight some uncomfortable archetypal elements behind the text which Shakespeare had attempted to iron out. *Measure for Measure* differs considerably from its sources in the absence of the more violent and sexual aspects found within the literary and folklore background to the story. Marowitz's production, it could be argued, went back from Shakespeare's play in order to emphasize the problematic issues in a more pertinent, effective manner. The director could not contemplate the presence of the romantic manipulator of the events. The Duke never appeared in the guise of the friar. This meant that Isabella was on her own, that she had no protector of any sort. In a permissive society it is often hard for students and audiences of the play to sympathize with Isabella's refusal to acquiesce to Angelo's proposal so as to save her brother's life. Marowitz's adaptation therefore took this possible modern objection to Isabella's conduct to its logical conclusion. In the absence of a Duke to whom she could turn for advice Isabella in her isolation was deliberately emphasized as being sexually repressed. Before committing herself to Angelo she fantasized both about her desire for his embraces and her immediate need for confession. She recoiled from the deed and yet in contradiction to the overt Shakespearean design, finally decided to sleep with the deputy. The decision being made she began to feel excited at the prospect of the night. In a symbolic scene Claudio embraced his sister in a lascivious, incestuous manner before leading her in the direction of Angelo's waiting arms. The deputy took her, stripped her naked and led her to his bed behind a huge parchment scroll proclaiming the resurrected law of Vienna. Her acquiescence throughout the scene was played with coy smiles and soft words. She was happy in her own release as well as that of her brother, but in the morning as she returned from the sexual adventure she casually uncovered an object in Angelo's study – and screamed, recognizing her brother's severed head. Although Marowitz faithfully employed the Shakespearean text he had rearranged passages, re-allocated speeches and words to different characters and excised much of the play to gain his effect. This was not Shakespeare's *Measure for Measure* nor was it meant to be. Rather it was Marowitz's dramatic interpretation of the play's sub-text whereby he exposed the themes behind Shakespeare's manipulation of the romance convention. A full understanding of the play's complexities looks behind and beyond the words to an understanding of motivation, symbol, allegory, psychology, archetype and total design. In such a study various problems are evident. That Mariana is substituted for Isabella in Angelo's bed might well suggest through correspondence and implication that in a real world outside the romantic techniques of the comic genre, Isabella's virginity would have been violated. Angelo's decision to execute Claudio despite the sacrifice of Isabella suggests too, without dramatic artificialities, that this in reality would have happened. A judge once corrupted will stop at nothing to cover his tracks even if it means his conscience will torment him. Angelo makes this clear in the text:

>   He should have liv'd;
> Save that his riotous youth, with dangerous sense,
> Might in the times to come have ta'en revenge
> By so receiving a dishonor'd life
> With ransom of such shame. Would yet he had lived.
> Alack, when once our grace we have forgot,
> Nothing goes right; we would, and we would not.
>   (IV. iv. 26–32)

Marowitz's idea, as with his previous Shakespearean adaptations, was to take the implications of the text and expose them with an awful naked clarity. Thereby he refused to allow Shakespeare's play to hide beneath conventions or popular expectations or traditional acting techniques, but abruptly transformed its progress to reveal what he saw as its essential statement. For some this proves an exciting approach to sacred texts preventing Shakespeare from fossilizing.[8] For others it reduces the dramatic sense of art and designed ambiguity and thus weakens effect. Either response demands, with a play such as *Measure for Measure*, serious consideration since the director exposes something ever present in the dramatic design but too often lost in the usual methods of approach.

The problems surrounding Isabella occur for both director and critic with her first appearance when as a novice entering the convent she declares her wish for 'a more strict restraint Upon the sisters stood, the votarists of Saint Clare' (I. iv. 4–5). That Isabella is portrayed as a novice is dramatically important in that it defines the reasons for her refusal to sacrifice her virginity. Nevertheless the question that seems to be explored in her portrayal as a nun is whether she is in fact mature enough to make decisions concerning her life, her spirituality and her sexuality. Thus the director and actress may legitimately ask if her desire for 'a more strict restraint' is illustrative of a rather immature romantic attitude to the cloisters or of a serious meditated desire to withdraw totally from the world in order to become closer to God. The immediate impression given by Paola Dionisotti on her appearance at the convent, suitcases in hand, in Barry Kyle's 1978 version, was that here was a woman who would never become a nun. For Stuart Burge however in 1976 Anna Calder Marshall appeared as an innocent who was later to realize the harshness of experience. Helen Mirren in contrast in Peter Gill's production was never seen in the nun's habit. Her decision for celibacy or sexuality was involved with an almost secular awareness of the dignity of her own being. Each interpretation in varying degrees finds a truth in the text as the play develops. In particular it finds a realization in her confrontations with Angelo. In a small-scale touring production for the National Theatre (Old Vic) in 1973/4 Jonathan Miller explored these scenes with a psychological insight. His modern dress production, with Angelo, Escalus and the Duke in pin-striped suits and Isabella in a twentieth-century knee length habit, was set in post-Freudian Vienna. Both nun and deputy were seen as sexually repressed so that their major confrontation was handled in 'neutral tones' as if they were attempting to 'dissociate themselves' from their own words. It consequently became an interview conducted from wooden utility chairs, across a table under which Angelo was able to fondle Isabella's knee before terminating the discussion 'by primly readjusting her skirt' (Irving Wardle, *The Times*, 24 November 1973). The very notion of sex had such an abhorrence to this Isabella that in her subsequent debate with Claudio (David Bradley) she became so irate as to strike him: a mixed reaction of both anger and fear.

The collision of sexual nausea and cold Puritanism also defined Estelle Kohler's Isabella and Ian Richardson's Angelo for the Barton production. Richardson, icy cold, slit-eyed, allowed the arrogance of Angelo's pride and hypocrisy to dictate his cruel proposal to Isabella. In the coldly perverted interview he advanced to her butting her with his groin. Only in solitude was he able to relax his act as he broke down in tears at the thought of his apostasy and inherent weaknesses. His pride was matched by an almost equal measure of the same sin on Isabella's side. F.R. Leavis has seen Isabella as possessing 'a kind of sensuality of martyrdom'.[9] Here it was displayed with a true measure of hysterical effrontery which was merely another facet of her moral exhibitionism. At the words 'More than our brother is our chastity' (II. iv. 184), as Harold Hobson noted (*The Sunday Times*, 5 April 1970), she thrust out her arm giving the martial impression that she would war to the end. Similarly John Barber (*Daily Telegraph*, 28 June 1976) noted the manner in which Anna Calder Marshall spoke the same line with great intensity at Edinburgh in 1976. This Isabella had a warm sonorous voice demonstrating her belief in her convictions. B.A. Young (*Financial Times*, 25 August 1976) pointed to her presentation of the words 'I have no superfluous leisure' as illustrative of the 'depth of her religious devotion'. Nevertheless as Barber commented she was able by deliberately contrasting strained facial expressions with the beauty of her diction to demonstrate that her piety was 'flawed by an hysterical self-righteousness'. Her Angelo, David Burke, was more brutish and comically exaggerated than Ian Richardson's cold Puritan, and so this humorous production lost a dimension in its presentation. The audience laughed too easily at him, finding little room for either horror or sympathy.

Francesca Annis's Isabella for Keith Hack's production was a woman cruelly placed in a nightmare world of sexual decadence. She could not conceive the extent or depth of the court degeneration. Vainly she fought against the odds, only to be overpowered time and again by the totality of the corruption: one final spot of purity to be enveloped and destroyed by the evil of the Viennese world. The forceful Helen Mirren provided an alternative portrayal for Peter Gill. Here was a determined Isabella whom Angelo (Patrick Drury) encountered at his peril, only his political power offering any form of protection. Miss Mirren's Isabella was a woman affronted by a male-dominated world. Her dignity as a human being was the price she was asked to pay and she refused to do so.

The most notable Angelo after Richardson, was that of Jonathan Pryce for Barry Kyle in 1978, since he presented a new slant on the character. His deputy from the start presented nervousness and frustration rather than cold hypocrisy. He was tense, worried, agitated, constantly moving and rubbing his hands together. It was an Angelo who had been placed in authority against his will. He felt as if the Duke had miscast him. He was uncomfortable and would inevitably fall. Some critics thought him too sympathetic for the dictates of the plot. There was a danger of this but the portrayal throughout was an intelligent attempt at seeing the complex psychological figure in a fresh and enlightening way. When David Suchet took over the role at the Aldwych in 1979, he imaginatively moved away from Pryce's interpretation to present an Angelo who grew in confidence after his appointment, so much so that although surprised at himself for falling in love,[10] he reaches a point where 'he even believes that to seduce a novice in a nunnery will be as easy as pronouncing a death sentence' (B.A. Young, *Financial Times*, 7 November 1979).

The progress of the interplay between the Duke, Isabella and Angelo culminates in the final recognition scene with the conventional comic arrangement of the multiple marriage: Angelo to Mariana, the Duke to Isabella, Lucio to his whore. The implications of the artificiality of this structured conclusion fascinated the directors throughout the decade. At one extreme was Marowitz. If we can discuss the relationship of correspondence between Isabella and Mariana to the extent whereby Mariana can be excised from the production, as occurred at The Open Space, a logical conclusion to the interpretation presents itself. For Marowitz Isabella had been reviled, prostituted and disappointed. Thus when she presented her case to the Duke on his return, he acted as the text states he might have done in real life. He refused to believe her and immediately had her imprisoned. The corollary to this action was a final cameo scene in which both Duke and Angelo revelled in their debauched hypocrisy mimicking some of the concluding lines of Shakespeare's design.[11] Although other directors did not go as far as Marowitz, they were keen to exploit variations in the ambiguity of the final action of the play:

Duke [to Isab.] If he be like your brother, for his sake
Is he pardon'd; and for your lovely sake
Give me your hand and say you will be mine.
He is my brother too: but fitter time for that. (v. i. 488–91)

It is a clear proposal to Isabella but she remains silent. Does this imply therefore that she does not willingly give her 'hand' as she certainly does not 'say' that she will be his? Is the Duke therefore rejected by Isabella since he has to repeat his proposal a few lines later?

Dear Isabel,
I have a motion much imports your good;
Whereto if you'll a willing ear incline,
What's mine is yours, and what yours is mine. (v. i. 531–4)

Again Isabella says nothing. Quite correctly directors are not slow to exploit such ambiguities in accordance with their creative presentation of the play. Anne Barton in her programme note for her husband's production suggested that it is 'at least possible that this silence is one of dismay.' Estelle Kohler's Isabella for John Barton therefore remained non-committal to the proposition thus embarrassing her Duke. For Jonathan Miller's production Gillian Barge went further. In her portrayal of a frigid Isabella she recoiled in horror repulsed by the very thought of the idea. The Duke was rejected. Anna Calder Marshall at the Edinburgh Festival remained alone on stage sadly contemplating the end of her spiritual aspirations as a nun. Slowly, meditatively, she removed her outer habit and walked in acquiescence to where the Duke had departed. The marriage, these directors implied, was a structural device which in being deliberately frustrated added a final dimension to the complex characterization of Isabella and to the play as a whole.

The way in which these three directors handled the marriage proposition in the last scene was indicative of a general approach to the drama whereby the traditional literary critical arguments concerning structural deficiencies or artificialities were negated in a desire to prove the work's appropriateness to a modern audience. John Barton noted that although on reading the play it is evident that a division in quality appears between the action preceding and following the confrontation between Isabella and Claudio, in rehearsal it disappeared:

> This is because the actors, if they have brought their characters to life in exploring the first half, can carry through that life into the play's more superficial resolution. I felt, in fact, that what seemed a problem in the study largely melted away in the theatre, when those characters were embodied by living actors.[12]

The practical decisions both of characterization and the need to find a consistency of interpretation for production largely relieved literary doubts about coherence. Once the director and his actors had found a core to the work which they could exploit, the critical debates and difficulties became lost in the theatrical purpose of their design. This, as we have seen, was determined by the relationship of the different principal actors to their roles but it was also seen in such areas as stage setting and in the relationship of the minor characters, Barnadine in particular, to the interpretations fostered by the directors.

In setting the play the designers for Barton, Miller, Hack and Kyle strictly limited the appearance of space so as to convey the claustrophobic incestuous nature of the corruption. Timothy O'Brien presented a closet effect for Barton's production with rear and side panels designed in a maze of cubes complemented by similarly symmetrical furniture for Angelo's study. All was close, cold and hypocritical. In a similar but even more claustrophobic vein Christopher Morley set Barry Kyle's production in a black box containing numerous doors, which would open stable-fashion to present whore-house or prison or full length to illustrate the executive nature of the deputy's office. Periodically overhead hung blind justice as an intermittent reminder of the theme. The black box was in some ways reminiscent of Sally Jacobs's white box setting for Peter Brook's *A Midsummer Night's Dream*, (1970); but the difference in colour was symptomatic of the thematic contrasts between the two plays. At the conclusion of the *Dream* the actors dressed in white jumped from the stage into the auditorium to shake hands with the audience in the joy and purity of the play's resolutions. In Kyle's *Measure for Measure*, however, the concluding episodes saw the fourth wall of the box rise from the floor down-stage to depict the gates of the city. Morley's Vienna was enclosed in the darkness of its own evils and intrigues. Despite gaining some self-knowledge the characters at the end of this play were still to re-enter their box rather than emerge from it. Thus the Kyle-Morley design fittingly fed off the earlier famous Brook-Jacobs idea so as to illustrate the repression of the one play in marked contrast to the release of the other. Such continuity in ideas tends to show the RSC at its best.[13]

Maria Björnson's design for Keith Hack's version also stressed the claustrophobic nature of the play. Vienna was realized in terms of a dark decaying brothel reminiscent of Genet's *The Balcony*. A large incongruous statue of the Madonna dominated an area of the stage, theatre lights protruded, a spiral staircase encumbered and rubbish cluttered. The whole was fretted with struts, girders and general stage properties and encompassed by a wire fence. We were in the dark hole of a prostituted state of stagnant sexuality. To the rear bare brick work was seen, and throughout actors strayed around the set, watching, sometimes applauding, sometimes bearing placards announcing 'whore', 'fornicator' or 'bawd'. Music by Stephen Oliver but in the style of Kurt Weill gave a further attempted Brechtian dimension to the total presentation. The characters looked like refugees from German Expressionism in their stylized whitened and generally grotesque make up. At the end of the play a trapeze flew in with the words *Deus ex Machina*. All was artificial and debauched. This was an indulgent, incestuous place ruled by the politics of fornication, hypocrisy and decadence. Bernard Culshaw's design for Jonathan Miller in the previous year was different. The claustrophobia in this set was clinically cold. The stage was divided half-prison and half-office with desk and hat stand. The music, not Kurt Weill but imitation Schöenberg, composed by Carl Davis, neatly emphasized the Viennese setting. Here was a producton, in design at least, which was to provide the cold intellectualism of sexual discovery and judicial hypocrisy. At times this Vienna, as one reviewer noted (Eric Shorter, *Daily Telegraph*, 24 November 1973), even presented the chill of East European totalitarianism fused with the foreboding atmosphere of 'sinister sexuality'.

In marked contrast to these designs were those for Stuart Burge and Peter Gill. Robin Archer's Elizabethan set in carved wood at Edinburgh was to double for Jonson's *The Devil is an Ass*. It cleverly allowed for the spatial elements of the Shakespearean theatre and yet simultaneously harmonized with the formal nonconformist interior of Edinburgh's Assembly Hall. Such a contrast of openness and intimate restriction seemed suited to the two Jacobean plays that were to produce their comedy from the misplaced humours of ambition and Puritanism. Peter Gill had different problems to solve at the Riverside Studios.[14] The vast expanse of the stage area at this theatre naturally prohibits a claustrophobic design. In earlier productions at the Studio which required intimate sets, such as Chekhov's *The Cherry Orchard*, Gill had made capital out of the space by a realization of strictly controlled movement. In his *Measure for Measure* however the movement lacked design. Many of the characters became lost, ambling, turning, walking to no particular place for no particular purpose. Occasionally however a focus was achieved, either through a wide visual angle such as at the moment of indignant, distraught Isabella's realization of Angelo's evil intent, or with a narrow angle as at the scene following the interval. A boy, spot-lighted down-stage, sang his song whilst Isabella and Mariana (Susan Brodrick) froze in conversation in the dimly lit area piled with cushions immediately behind him. The innocence of the voice complemented the reality of the words and the experience of statuesque women. The rear wall had one strip of wood panel about head-high and the floor was given a brick effect.[15] Otherwise there was little decor in a production that consequently relied heavily on the language. This was poorly executed by some of the actors. A directorial plan, therefore which, on numerous occasions attempted to capitalize on the fact that no proscenium arch separated the actors from the auditorium, by having his characters talk directly to the audience, was frustrated. The costumes as in the majority of the productions – the exceptions being Miller's and Hack's – were traditionally Elizabethan-Jacobean.

At The Open Space, Robin Don employed symbols in his design for Marowitz: the parchment of the law, the red chair of office, the bed, the red glow of the lights for the prostitute scene, all reminded an audience contained in jury box seats, of the corrupt nature of the trial they witnessed. Juxtapositioning of the text and the redesigned scene structure allowed the director to achieve some intellectually effective moments as for example when the 'Be prepared for death' speech was delivered by a newly-created character, the Bishop, to Claudio at the moment of the brother's execution and of Angelo's simultaneous violation of Isabella's ironically willing body.

The Lucios of the decade correctly reflected or drew out further the particular themes of the various productions. Terence Hardiman was 'rat-like' in 1970, Barry Stanton like a seedy 'stage manager' in 1974, David Suchet, a 'common vulgarian' in 1976 and John Nettles an accomplished spiv bordering on the foppish in 1979.[16] The most interesting variations in a minor character were found in Barnadine. Both Anthony Langdon and David Waller played the part for John Barton as a drunken dissolute, urinating into a chamber pot which subsequently had a crucifix thrust into it, before being finally emptied over his head. The Christian ethics of this hypocritical Puritanical state were beneath ridicule for a man such as Barnadine. They were merely part of the crude banality of existence. Dan Meaden in the part for Keith Hack spoke from off stage, his voice being amplified into the auditorium through loud speakers. When he did appear he also illustrated himself as the natural dregs of a corrupt civilization, baring his behind and breaking wind at the spectators. In 1978 Barry Kyle began the season by having his Barnadine, Conrad Asquith, enter naked from his cell. Whatever the idea behind this was it failed to work as neither the critics nor the audience realized or appreciated the intention. After a few weeks Barnadine was given a loin cloth. In Edinburgh in 1976 David Foxxe's Barnadine showed a mock dignity in dusting his seat before sitting, an idea which was taken further by Robert Hamilton for Peter Gill in 1979. Hamilton's Barnadine emerged from his prison head held high and back straight. He brushed down his clothes in an effort to keep control of both his thoughts and his self-respect. His decision not to be executed came not from a degenerate but from a rational mind that had nothing in common with the thoughts or plans of the other characters. It was a decision given with a competent rather than a drunken finality but one which still emphasized his separateness and his refreshing ability to illustrate the fallibility of the duke.

The question why *Measure for Measure* was so popular throughout the seventies on the British stage, can perhaps only be answered by seeing, as the directors attempted to do, its appropriateness to western society. A play dealing in the hypocrisy, corruption and shallowness of government was not out of place in the age of Vietnam and Watergate, Northern Ireland and Poulson.[17] In its emphasis on the bankruptcy of law and order, and in its exposure of the impotence of both lax and over-rigid governmental controls it may also have appealed to a society attempting to regain its economic and political stability. The directors sometimes made us laugh with the play, sometimes shocked us with it, sometimes forced us to consider and enter its moral debates. A definitive production did not appear but perhaps could not do so since the potential instability of the society which was to produce it may have been too closely related to the inherent ambiguities that the play naturally contains. In its complexity *Measure for Measure* proved to be a rich play for an uneasy decade.

6 The Changeling

It has been wryly said of the beauty and the beast fable that the prince's transformation into the frog is obnoxious to all but the frogs who see it as a definite improvement. This sentiment, with some qualification, may well be understood in the context of Middleton and Rowley's *The Changeling*. Robert Jordan has demonstrated the mythic qualities of the play and the reversal of its beauty and the beast conclusion.[1] Whereas the fable ends with the frog returning to his true state as the handsome prince, the drama twists the situation 'to reveal that the princess is in fact a beast'.[2] It has to be asked further however to whom it is that she appears as a beast. It is certainly not to De Flores since Beatrice has provided him with an ecstasy and purpose of existence. Her bestiality is rather one perceived by herself and the Alicante society to which she belongs:

> *Alsemero*   You are a whore!
> *Beatrice*   What a horrid sound it hath!
>   It blasts a beauty to deformity;
>   Upon what face soever that breath falls,
>   It strikes it ugly: oh you have ruin'd
>   What you can ne'er repair again. (v. iii. 31–5)[3]

If the name of whore denotes ugliness how much more degrading is the deed and its companion, murder. The irony however is deeper than this since from the De Flores viewpoint such statements of deformity are ridiculous. For the servant Beatrice-Joanna's action has liberated her from such terms which are representative of the bourgeois constraints of the civilization to which she once belonged. He has transformed her by capitalizing on her inherent selfishness so as to enable her to join him in what he regards to be the purpose of his life and the logic of his own system of ethics. In opposition to the practices of the society in which he serves, De Flores creates an existence for himself and his love which he sees as meaningful even in its destruction:

> ... her honour's prize
> Was my reward; I thank life for nothing
> But that pleasure: it was so sweet to me
> That I have drunk up all, left none behind
> For any man to pledge me. (v. iii. 167–71)

It is through such an existentialist philosophy that De Flores retains a personal credibility throughout the play. It is the hallmark of his individualism in conflict with a society from which by class, position and physical disfigurement he is totally alienated. In Alicante Vermandero's servant is regarded no higher than a dumb working animal. His worth is judged not by any personal, spiritual or inner qualities but by his usefulness as a servant ready to retrieve a dropped glove as a puppy might fetch his master's slippers:

> *Vermandero* Look, girl, thy glove's fall'n
> Stay, stay, – De Flores, help a little. (i. i. 225–6)

He is merely patronized by his superiors who smile upon him and then disregard him as an irrelevance doing his duty well.[4] For a spoilt daughter such as Beatrice-Joanna, however, the servant provides the ugly fascination of a creature from a different order of life:

> Mischief on your officious forwardness!
> Who bade you stoop? They touch my hand no more:
> There, for t'other's sake I part with this,
> *[Takes off the other glove and throws it down]*
> Take 'em and draw thine own skin off with 'em. (i. i. 227–30)

The sensuality of delight in Beatrice-Joanna's conduct is often noted. She is the sadistic child who at first kicks the puppy and then at a whim toys and teases him for her personal desire:

> And now I think on one: I was to blame,
> I ha' marr'd so good a market with my scorn;
> 'T had been done questionless; the ugliest creature

>   Creation fram'd for some use, yet to see
>   I could not mark so much where it should be! (II. ii. 41–5)

She thinks only in terms of markets, use and creatures. For her life is a matter of buying and selling. If the arranged husband proves to be unsuitable further arrangements have to be made to replace him. Such a dog-faced animal as De Flores was made for such a purpose. Beatrice consequently is the product of the mercantile society in which she lives,[5] a society totally divorced from any spirituality. The first irony of the play is that she meets Alsemero in the temple, for religion has no meaningful place in this society. Beatrice's concept of a spiritual plane can only be either of statues bought as pretty ornaments or of an invisible world of guardians to be employed and discarded when they prove no longer attractive. Men are consequently described as of the same order, satisfying superficial whims worked as servants or chosen as husbands from the shelf, like figurines from the piety stall.[6] The only trouble with the husbands however is that once chosen they assume superior rights to the wife in society. They willingly put themselves in the shop window but with an affidavit that demands fidelity.[7] It is this which Tomazo feels Alonzo has forgotten in his infatuation with the girl:

>   Unsettle your affection with all speed
>   Wisdom can bring it to, your peace is ruin'd else.
>   Think what a torment 'tis to marry one
>   Whose heart is leap'd into another's bosom:
>   If ever pleasure she receives from thee,
>   It comes not in thy name, or of thy gift;
>   She lies but with another in thine arms,
>   He the half-father unto all thy children
>   In the conception ... (II. i. 129–37)

Taken to its extreme it is precisely this fear that results in Alsemero's marital alchemy, a portable laboratory to test the fidelity of his bargain as a smith might try the temper of his gold. Marriage is about bargaining not about love. The partners prove to be possessions. Thus in the final act Beatrice struggles confusedly to keep her man, confessing the murder rather than the fornication, whilst he, resembling the later Soranzo in *'Tis Pity She's a Whore* bullies her to find out her real worth:

> I'll all demolish, and seek out truth within you,
> If there be any left ... (v. iii. 36-7)

Pathetically she proves to have been the bad bargain which he arrogantly claims to have always been his suspicion,

> 'Twas in my fears at first, 'twill have it now:
> Oh, thou art all deform'd! (v. iii. 76-7)

This is the bourgeois society of the play in which De Flores is the menial. It is a world of selfish will and judgement,[8] of protection and pettiness, a society dedicated to the preservation of the self at all costs. Vermandero's first conversation with Alsemero defines the attitude:

> *Vermandero* ... I must know
>   Your country; we use not to give survey
>   Of our chief strengths to strangers; our citadels
>   Are plac'd conspicuous to outward view,
>   On promonts' tops; but within are secrets.
> *Alsemero*   A Valencian, sir.
> *Vermandero*   A Valencian?
>   That's native sir; of what name, I beseech you?
> *Alsemero*   Alsemero, sir.
> *Vermandero*   Alsemero; not the son
>   Of John de Alsemero?
> *Alsemero*   The same, sir
> *Vermandero*   My best love bids you welcome. (I. i. 162-71)

We might well briefly wonder what the reception would have been if the young man had not been the son of John de Alsemero. Connection, country, social contact, class, determine acceptance into a society not altogether different from our own. Priorities in Alicante are the defence of the city and the social structure at all costs just as the modern world indulges in its arms race and attempts to keep its status quo, West or East financing its social, sporting and cultural activities whilst starvation proves the norm in parts of Africa, India and Asia. Alicante is a microcosm of social conduct and civilization, a society rarely questioning itself since, like its own Beatrice-Joanna, it is confident and safe in the knowledge of its own goodness.

Thus the conclusion of the play demonstrates Beatrice's sin to be one of rebellion against social regulations and propriety rather than against a spiritual concept of moral good. A victim of her society as well as herself she enters in the final scene to confess her deeds still ignorant of their cause. Thus her speech 'Oh come not near me, sir, I shall defile you' (v. iii. 149f.) proves to be pitifully ironic. As we might expect defilement is seen by the father not in terms of spirituality nor even of blood but of social reputation. As the daughter dies his words are only of himself:

> Oh, my name is enter'd now in that record
> Where till this fatal hour 'twas never read. (v. iii. 180–1)

This is the signal for the Alicante society to reassure itself of its inherent bourgeois strength. From these words on, the bodies of De Flores and Beatrice-Joanna are ignored in the platitudinous sentia uttered by the characters remaining. They move to the front of the stage in order to pledge themselves to the status quo of the civilization under challenge. Patronizingly and conceitedly they console each other in their pretentious wisdom with Alsemero finally and sentimentally affirming his position of filial obligation:

> Sir, you have yet a son's duty living,
> Please you, accept it; let that your sorrow
> As it goes from your eye, go from your heart;
> Man and his sorrow at the grave must part. (v. iii. 216–19)

For a modern audience at least the sentiment of this conclusion confirms the negativism of the play's action. Deaths may have occurred, the human psyche probed and a grotesque existentialist challenge to the society delivered, but for Alsemero, Vermandero and the rest nothing has been learnt. The same should not however be said of the audience. We should have perceived a fable bringing from the deepest recesses of the human condition an attack on the mediocrity of Alicante civilization and its veneered evaluation of life. The perception of this hollow society, however is not something foisted on the drama by an exterior appreciation of social abuse but is rather ever-present in the play's technique and structure. In the main plot, as many critics have demonstrated, the authors deliberately undercut social pretension and confidence through the use of pun and irony.[9] This constantly occurs in the exchanges between De Flores and Beatrice-Joanna which from the beginning are littered with sexual innuendo. Ironic undercutting is common throughout the play and is seen with most of the characters. Thus in v. iii. for example Vermandero and Alsemero each certain he has identified Alonzo's murderer, confront one another in a ridiculous non-communicative exchange:

> *Vermandero* Oh, Alsemero, I have a wonder for you.
> *Alsemero* No, sir, 'tis I, I have a wonder for you.
> *Vermandero* I have suspicion near as proof itself
>   For Piracquo's murder.
> *Alsemero*   Sir, I have proof
>   Beyond suspicion for Piracquo's murder.
> *Vermandero* Beseech you, hear me; these two have been disguised
>   E'er since the deed was done.
> *Alsemero*   I have two other
>   That were more close disguis'd than your two could be
>   E'er since the deed was done.
> *Vermandero* You'll hear me! – these mine own servants –
> *Alsemero* Hear me; – those nearer your servants,
>   That shall acquit them, and prove them guiltless.
> *Franciscus* That may be done with easy truth, sir.
> *Tomazo* How is my cause bandied through your delays!
>   (v. iii. 121-34)

Theatrically, of course, this dialogue allows for an ironic interlude before the recognition scene and thus helps to build a dramatic tension. It does so however by focusing on each man's inability to listen to the other as the one wallows in the pride and knowledge of his discovery, whilst the other bandies words in his growing exasperation. Pride consequently allows the subject to be circumscribed rather than revealed with even the dead man's brother – a continual source of irritation to Vermandero's self-satisfaction at Beatrice's marriage to Alsemero – being ignored. In this world people do not count, the importance of the truth, the humanity of the brother, the very nature of Alonzo's disappearance and death being in effect of little consequence. Superficiality reigns supreme. This is the futility of Alicante existence rightfully reflected in the absurdity of dialogue. The dangerous vacuity of the civilization is also well-demonstrated through the use of the sub-plot. The critical arguments for the relevance or not of the madhouse scenes have been largely settled by scholars.[10] The lunatic asylum is in correspondence with the castle. The inmates are to perform at the feast and the castle's servants disguise themselves to enter the world of the madmen. Isabella parallels Beatrice-Joanna as Lollio distortedly reflects De Flores. The lessons learnt in the asylum however are not easy to perceive. In the final scene the sub-plot characters like those in the main plot, cover up all in the general denouement dedicated to the re-establishment of social sanity but their words prove to be innocently tame in comparison with the actions that have preceded them:

> *Antonio* ... I was chang'd too, from a little ass as I was, to a great fool as I am, and had like to ha' been chang'd to the gallows, but that you know my innocence always excuses me.
> *Franciscus* I was chang'd from a little wit to be stark mad, Almost for the same purpose.
> *Isabella* Your change is still behind, But deserve best your transformation:
> You are a jealous coxcomb, keep schools of folly,
> And teach your scholars how to break your own head.
> *Alibius* I see all apparent, wife, and will change now Into a better husband, and never keep
> Scholars that shall be wiser than myself. (v. iii. 204–15)

There is of course some truth in what is said. They all have learnt their lessons especially in being brought so close to the gallows. The scenes in the asylum however were more comically hideous in their teaching than is here admitted. The madhouse allows the play a series of tableaux ridiculing both the romantic poet and the chivalrous lover by expressing their art in the anarchy of uncontrolled sexuality and sterile subservience. This first becomes apparent in III. iii., where the poet Franciscus both verbally and visually presents the degradation into which sanity has fallen. Speaking of Titania and Oberon, of 'daisies, primrose, violets' (III. iii. 48–52) he is soon compelled into a position of humiliation. The whip forces him on all-fours ready and willing to be mounted by his keeper Lollio. Released from this debasement he imaginatively transforms himself into a Tiresian woman so as to make a sexual attack on the servant, raving absurdly and sadistically of the moon and the demons of the night:

> Luna is now big-bellied, and there's room
> For both of us to ride with Hecate;
> I'll drag thee up into her silver sphere,
> And there we'll kick the dog, and beat the bush,
> That barks against the witches of the night:
> The swift lycanthropi that walks the round,
> We'll tear their wolvish skins, and save the sheep.
> *[Tries to seize Lollio]* (III. iii. 79–85)

The dramatic scope here is considerable as Franciscus stalks his keeper, raving of the madness of the night, before attempting his assault. The condition of the animal is evoked by Rowley as the madman is subdued again by the whip. The insanity of love has to be curbed by the rope's end just as in society it is controlled by the marital conventions of the market place. It is exactly this that the other lover, Antonio, does not understand but which Isabella firmly comprehends. If she is unfaithful to her husband, however ridiculous, obnoxious or cruel he may be, she exposes herself to the gaze and use of all that might desire her:

> *Lollio* One thing I must tell you mistress: you perceive that I am privy to your skill; if I find you minister once and set up trade, I put in for my thirds, I shall be mad or fool else.
> *Isabella* The first place is thine, believe it, Lollio
>   If I do fall –
> *Lollio* I fall upon you.
> *Isabella* So. (IV. iii.34–41)

The demands Antonio is making upon Isabella are ones which in the dressage of Alicante behaviour have a natural conclusion in disgrace. Nevertheless if he is serious in his passion there is an alternative which in its anarchy disregards the demands of society. If he desires unrestrained love then Isabella is willing to provide it with an intensity that his bourgeois sensitivity is unable to accept. At IV. iii. 102, Isabella enters as a madwoman to give herself totally to Antonio if he is willing to take her in the lunacy of sexual violence to which Franciscus has alluded. Rehearsing the wedding dance Antonio is knocked to the floor by the woman, 'He's down, he's down, what a terrible fall he had!' She straddles him commanding him to rise, 'Stand up, thou son of Cretan Dedalus', but as he wriggles to free himself she joins him on the floor '... let us tread the lower labyrinth;/I'll bring thee to the clue' (IV. iii. 102–8). Together they struggle, Antonio attempting to get free, confusedly pleading 'Prithee, coz, let me alone' whilst Isabella continues in the sexual vehemence of her act. She rolls with him, caresses him, and physically embarrasses him in her sexual madness:

> A crook'd chamelion-colour'd rainbow hung
> Like a tiara down unto thy hams.
> Let me suck out those billows in thy belly;
> Hark how they roar and rumble in the straits! (IV. iii. 113–6)

Desperately he attempts to free himself, 'Pox upon you, let me alone!' but she perseveres in her lasciviousness, key words 'mount', 'moon', 'wild rebellious waves', 'drown'd', 'love' accompanying the physicality of her embraces:

> Why shouldst thou mount so high as Mercury,
> Unless thou hadst reversion to his place?
> Stay in the moon with me, Endymion,
> And we will rule these wild rebellious waves,
> That would have drown'd my love. (IV. iii. 119–23)

Her bestiality proves too great for the constraints of his middle-class mentality and thus Antonio, like Icarus, finds he cannot climb as high as he desired. Degenerately he turns to the threat of violence to protect his self-interest and esteem in an unknowing but inevitable rejection of his proclaimed desire:

> I'll kick thee if again thou touch me,
> Thou wild unshapen antic; I am no fool,
> You bedlam! (IV. iii. 124–6)

Antonio's romantic revolution has been a pretence. He is

impotent in the anarchy of love and is rightly dismissed by Isabella. All that can be left for him and Franciscus are the platitudes of reconciliation and remorse paralleling those found in the main plot. Like Alsemero and Vermandero they profess an understanding but, as with their superiors, it is tragically one limited by their condition rather than freed by their experience.

It would however be incorrect to over-redress the balance in the play so as to see Middleton and Rowley in support of De Flores's existentialism or Isabella's anarchy at the expense of the Alicante community. The dramatists' vision is not didactic. It is one presented as an experience for the audience to stimulate ideas rather than to answer problems. Thus Isabella can demonstrate an awareness of intense passion which is seemingly contradicted by her part in the scene, whilst De Flores can equally follow viciousness with a tenderness of words as at the end of III. iv:

> Come, rise, and shroud your blushes in my bosom; *[Raises her]*
> Silence is one of pleasure's best receipts:
> Thy peace is wrought for ever in this yielding.
> 'Las how the turtle pants! Thou'lt love anon
> What thou so fear'st and faint'st to venture on. (III. iv. 167–71)

This example of 'one of Middleton's most daring and most perfectly managed modulations of feeling'[11] provides the audience with the jarring sense of incongruity that dominates the play. At once we are to realize his abhorrent brutality and yet his honest belief in the truth of his love. Although we see him standing in front of us physically and spiritually deformed we know that by his own standards he is a very different being from the way we or the Alicante civilization see him. His answer in murder, rape and suicide, to the shallow society in which he lives, is not one presented by the authors to be followed but it is rather an exposé of the follies among which he lives. Thus in *The Changeling* as in earlier plays like *The Revenger's Tragedy* and *Volpone*, we are presented with a theatrical experience of the sterility that may be the human condition. Both the individual and social conduct of the play's characters prove to be abhorrent. No answers are given to the problems presented since they can only be seen and understood. It is here that we find the play's thematic purpose one which as with Jonson's *Volpone*, is stressed in the epilogue through the actor's self conscious reference to theatrical artifice:

> All we can do to comfort one another,
> To stay a brother's sorrow for a brother,
> To dry a child from the kind father's eyes,
> Is to no purpose, it rather multiplies;
> Your only smiles have power to cause re-live
> The dead again, or in their rooms to give
> Brother a new brother, father a child;
> If these appear, all griefs are reconciled. (v. iii. 220-27)

Art merely represents. Cures have to be accomplished outside the theatre doors.

The play has rightly been presented with some regularity on the post-war British stage, four productions being seen in 1978–9 alone. Of these, two London presentations found prominence. Staged within a few months of each other by Peter Gill at the Riverside Studios and Terry Hands at the Aldwych they begged comparison and initiated some interesting debate. Gill's strength lay in his handling of the madness scenes. The Riverside Studio is large with raked seating formed on scaffolding. The lunatics seemed always to be beneath this and therefore below the audience, howling, banging and running on to the stage to make the scene changes. Franciscus's (Paul Kember) disguise was properly effeminate whilst Antonio (Robert Lindsay), yoyo in hand, sniffed, scratched and squinted before a closely cropped Lollio (David Troughton). Isabella (Sharon Duce) retained a dignity throughout, passing Beatrice (Emma Piper) during one scene change, as a ghost of what the heroine might have been. As the two women crossed with just the slightest glance at each other one felt the chill of the play and understood the superficiality of the supposed beauty. The dumb show was well conveyed with flashing lights, illuminating brief ordered tableaux of the marriage, the ghost and the unsuspecting, frightened De Flores (Brian Cox). The back drop was of four panels on which David Lawes portrayed elongated bodies pulled towards disfigurement. The floor was paved with flagstones allowing the echo of soldiers' boots or madmen's feet. As in Gill's *Measure for Measure* the vast expanse of the stage was either sensitively constricted or used to the full as the need determined through the lighting.

Thus a claustrophobic atmosphere was created, for example, as De Flores channelled Alonzo (Joseph Blatchley) around a stage transformed into the dark narrow passages of the castle. Movement was well-disciplined, actors at key moments watching and circling each other creating a precarious tension. The madmen were in pastel green and yellow, Franciscus with a wreath about his brow. The servants and soldiers wore martial grey whilst De Flores and Lollio were dressed in brown and Vermandero in black with a gold chain of office. A brown hat partly covered De Flores's ulcerated face, ugly but possibly not quite horrific enough. It was sufficiently vile however to produce the necessary audience reaction as Beatrice fingered it, played with his hair and even pursed her lips in tempting him to murder. In III. iv. Beatrice in a purple robe, her golden hair loose about her head pleadingly held on to De Flores's leg only to be dragged screaming about the floor as in contempt he moved from her. Brian Cox's servant truly had the fascination and cruelty of evil. He was a man with whom no maid should have dallied.

Emrys James played the same role for Terry Hands. Mr. James is an accomplished stage malcontent, his Iago to Brewster Mason's Othello in 1971 being one of the most memorable portrayals of the part in recent years. For De Flores however he was a little meditative, too Iago-like, leaning against the sides of the stage contemplating his evil from beneath a black mask covering half of his face. The dominant colours of Hands's production were blood red and black in a 'geometric constructivist design of giant movable pincers, crossbeamed with girders' (Rosemary Say, *Sunday Telegraph*, 22 October 1978). The emphasis throughout was on the emergence of horrific sexual forces within the shallowness of the society. Thus at the dumb show a cardboard replica of Beatrice was married to Alsemero as the real woman upstage was grotesquely 'serviced' by De Flores from the rear. No pun was allowed to escape. The verbal wit was stressed to its very limit. From the start Beatrice-Joanna was seen as sexually repressed and thus in tempting De Flores she offered her bosom rather than her lips for his enjoyment. Some critics felt that whereas Gill had managed to convey a dream-like surrealism in his production, Hands's had allowed for too much melodrama and sensationalism, thus dangerously reducing a serious work of art to the regions bordering on the banal.[12]

Others felt in opposition, that he had well conveyed the tenor of the drama, found essentially in the humour of the pun and verbal play.[13] Each production seen within the space of six months strangely allowed the totality of the Caroline work to come to the fore. Peter Gill, in particular, demonstrated an ability to fuse the two plots into a surrealist and cogent whole forcing its sense of sterility from the stage into the auditorium.

Earlier productions of *The Changeling* at the Royal Court in 1961 and the Royal Lyceum Edinburgh in 1970 were influenced by Goya's Spain. The programme note for the Edinburgh production directed by Richard Eyre with Anna Calder Marshall as Beatrice and David Burke as De Flores stated:

> In *The Changeling*, as in Goya's etchings, love is seen at best as a kind of 'tame madness' – to be in love is to become a changeling; at its worst, it becomes an uncontrollable force which gives birth to insane demons who mercilessly manipulate their progenitors and whose purification lies only in death.

Tony Richardson's production at the Royal Court employed the flamboyance of Spanish colour and costume allowing Robert Shaw's unkempt De Flores to stand out as an ugly, tight-lipped malcontent dominating a production which correctly attempted to fuse the two plots.[14] The more recent provincial productions of the plays at Bristol Old Vic directed by Adrian Noble in 1978 and at the Victoria Theatre, Stoke-on-Trent, directed by Kate Crutchley in 1979 were straightforward, well depicting the forceful drama but avoiding the cruel farce of the Aldwych or the emotional nightmare of the Riverside. One other significant production however should be noted. In 1974 the BBC presented the play on television with Helen Mirren as Beatrice and Stanley Baker as De Flores. An outstanding feature of this experiment was the way in which the close proximity and intensity of the work was achieved because of the dictates of the small screen.[15]

In the live theatre the small auditorium would no doubt produce a similar effect. *The Changeling* was written for a private theatre and the conciseness of image in both its poetry and its visual symbols may well reward the confines of a studio more than a large auditorium. Certainly plays such as *The Maid's Tragedy* and *'Tis Pity She's a Whore* have achieved considerable success in such houses.[16]

7 'Tis Pity She's a Whore

The apparent inadequacies and seemingly central irrelevancy of *'Tis Pity She's a Whore* for a modern audience are such as by right we may wonder why it still retains its popularity. Critics[1] have been uneasy about its place in the canon of Elizabethan plays and with T.S. Eliot some have agreed that it is not Ford's best work.[2] Its most recent production by BBC television in 1980, clearly did not trust the appropriateness of the text for the twentieth-century and radically changed both plot and diction to make a highly praised television drama but something remote from Ford's play. Its last stage production, at the RSC's studio theatre in 1978, was praised by Michael Billington as overcoming audience indifference or even sympathy towards incest by pushing the work 'in the direction of black comedy rather than moral melodrama' (*The Guardian*, 22 July 1977). In addition Brian Morris, one of the text's three major editors[3] in recent times, has quoted anthropological evidence demonstrating modern society's lack of interest in the drama's central emblem. Yet all this has occurred with a play which together with Ford's other works, caused Havelock Ellis at the turn of the century to proclaim him as the most modern of the Jacobeans.[4] Possibly in response to this critical evaluation of Ford some of the play's directors over the last ten years, have interestingly set the play in the early twentieth-century imposing upon it an Edwardian atmosphere of a thinly veneered outward respectability disguising a strongly diseased interior. Some academic critics[5] have similarly continued Ellis's line stressing Ford's appropriateness in the company of late-nineteenth-century and twentieth-century writers. Others, however, have found such an approach restrictive and have therefore attempted to gain a fuller perspective.[6] This can be realized by a return to the text. There we find that some areas, seemingly deficient at first acquaintance, are the play's strength. In them lies its theme and vision. Its modernity proves to be Ford's recognition, as applicable to the 1980s as to the 1890s or the 1630s, of a sterile, self-destructive world; one which he describes through the sexual relationship of the brother and sister as impotent and ineffective members of an incestuously structured and minded society.

A central problem of *'Tis Pity* is that, with the possible exception of Annabella, few of its characters engage our sympathy. Giovanni does not have the metaphysical stature of Dr Faustus nor the existentialist integrity of De Flores.[7] Certainly he defines himself in existential terms:

> O, the glory
> Of two united hearts like hers and mine!
> Let poring book-men dream of other worlds,
> My world, and all of happiness, is here,
> And I'd not change it for the best to come:
> A life of pleasure is Elysium. (v. iii. 11–16)

– but his rebellion is too self-conscious in that he and Annabella constantly want to be both rebels from and yet accepted members of the Parma society. Their sin is not outrageous in its initial challenge but shallow in that it attempts to replace convention by a shadow of itself. The opening discussion with the Friar is not an intellectual debate over the rights or wrongs of the deed since Giovanni's arguments express the very reasons why he should not bed his sister:

> Say that we had one father, say one womb
> (Curse to my joys!) gave both us life and birth;
> Are we not therefore each to other bound
> So much the more by nature? by the links
> Of blood, of reason? nay, if you will have't,
> Even of religion, to be ever one,
> One soul, one flesh, one love, one heart, one *all*? (I. i. 28–34)

The rhetoric demands a negative response. This is the inadequate reasoning of the immature, phrased to illustrate the peevishness of the youth. It is further developed in his proposal to his sister where the lies so easily told will expose the pretensions of his erroneous version of Neo-Platonism:

> Wise Nature first in your creation meant
> To make you mine: else't had been sin and foul
> To share one beauty to a double soul.
> Nearness in birth or blood doth but persuade
> A nearer nearness in affection.
> I have asked counsel of the holy Church,
> Who tells me I may love you, and 'tis just
> That since I may, I should; and will, yes, will ... (I. ii. 236–43)

This is the philosophy of a man incapable of facing the commitment of his sin. Misapplying theories of beauty and then proceeding to lie to gain his ends, he demonstrates his hollowness.[8] Unlike De Flores he cannot engage in total rebellion. He looks for permission and not receiving it invents it for himself. He then conjures up a system of values in his atheism by which he and his sister might live in their sin without conscience. It is a mode of conduct absurdly paralleling the sacramental conventions of society, inventing even a marriage ritual to justify the incestuous union:

> *Annabella* On my knees, *[She kneels.]*
> Brother, even by our mother's dust, I charge you,
> Do not betray me to your mirth or hate:
> Love me, or kill me, brother.
> *Giovanni* On my knees, *[He kneels.]*
> Sister, even by my mother's dust I charge you,
> Do not betray me to your mirth or hate:
> Love me, or kill me, sister. (I. ii. 253–9)

He receives her ring (II. iv. 35–41) and demands their total commitment to each other:

> *Giovanni* But tell me, sweet, canst thou be dared to swear
> That thou wilt live to me, and to no other?
> *Annabella* By both our loves I dare ... (II. i. 26–8)

Thus when to save her reputation and her soul the Friar suggests marriage as a solution, Giovanni indignantly objects:

> Marriage? Why, that's to damn her; that's to prove
> Her greedy of variety of lust. (II. v. 41–2)

Paradoxically marriage would force either an admission of or an act of sin. If Annabella accepted the Christian sacrament in good faith then the incest would be admitted. Yet if she were to marry for social reputation then too sin would occur, the sin of adultery against their arbitrary ritual of commitment.[9] She accepts the latter and is punished for it:

> What danger's half so great as thy revolt?
> Thou art a faithless sister .... (v. v. 8–9)

She has offended and in his atheism Giovanni can only revenge by forging the final parallel with Christianity. He has become as God:

> ...why, I hold fate
> Clasped in my fist, and could command the course
> Of time's eternal motion; hadst thou been
> One thought more steady than an ebbing sea. (v. v. 11–14)

The action of his fantasy from here takes its course. Annabella has sinned against him and therefore retribution has to be made. He justifies her murder in terms of a deific sacrifice. Vengeance belongs neither to God nor society but to Giovanni:

> Annabella   What means this?
> Giovanni   To save thy fame, and kill thee in a kiss. *[Stabs her.]*
>   Thus die, and die by me, and by my hand:
>   Revenge is mine; honour doth love command. (v. v. 83–6)

Later he implies that this act was as great as that made on Calvary:

> The glory of my deed
> Darkened the mid-day sun, made noon as night. (v. vi. 21–2)

It of course did no such thing. Standing before the birthday feast bloodied heart in hand Giovanni is not the successor of Jesus pointing to his Sacred Heart but rather a reminder of the common executioner disembowelling his victims at Tyburn.[10] The dramatist however allows the poignancy of the Annabella sacrifice to take precedence over the grotesque. Although an apostate to their love her repentance demonstrates a vulnerability that allows her to retain an appealing innocence through experience. Thus her replies to the brother emphasize the purity of the oblation:

> Then I see your drift;
> Ye blessed angels, guard me!
>
> O brother, by your hand?
>
> Forgive him, Heaven – and me my sins; farewell
> Brother, unkind, unkind – mercy, great
> Heaven! – O – O! *[Dies]* (v. v. 66–7, 87, 92–3)

The sacrificial victim follows the Christian pattern in appealing only to the heavens for help and then in forgiving the agent of death in his act of cruelty. She consequently cements an audience sympathy which, because of her treatment earlier by Soranzo and her general confusion throughout the later part of the play, has been steadily allowed to develop.

Giovanni plays his act out to the end. Refusing the Cardinal's advice 'yet to cry to Heaven' (v. vi. 103) he turns not to God but to death:

> Death, thou art a guest long looked-for, I embrace
> Thee and thy wounds; O, my last minute comes.
> Where'er I go, let me enjoy this grace,
> Freely to view my Annabella's face. (v. vi. 103-7)

The emphasis however is not on a rejection of the Cardinal's values but on his plea that wheresoever death takes him he might again see his sister. This is the Giovanni that has been presented throughout the play, ready to believe in anything, atheism or Christianity, if it allows his love.[11] Thus in v. v. he shows himself ready to embrace concepts of heaven and hell if they mean he will not lose her totally:

> *Giovanni*   ... could I believe
> This might be true, I could believe as well

There might be Hell or Heaven.
Annabella   That's most certain.
Giovanni   A dream, a dream: else in this other world
We should know one another.
Annabella   So we shall
Giovanni   Have you heard so?
Annabella   For certain,
Giovanni   But d'ee think
That I shall see you there, you look on me;
May we kiss one another, prate or laugh,
Or do as we do here?
Annabella   I know not that ... (v. v. 33–41)

These are the ravings of the unbalanced mind as the protagonist prepares to make his sacrifice, and they help show a confusion that is continued to the very moment of the murder where immediately before he makes himself into a demi-god, he still begs her to pray to Heaven:

Pray, Annabella, pray; since we must part,
Go thou white in soul, to fill a throne
Of innocence and sanctity in Heaven.
Pray, pray, my sister. (v. v. 63–6)

Inconsistencies such as this help Ford to undermine Giovanni's fantasies but throughout the dramatist allows a variety of further perspectives to satirize his protagonist's position. Thus immediately following his heated accusations that the Friar's superstitions have betrayed him:

'Fore Heaven, you make
Some petty devil factor 'twixt my love
And your religion-maskèd sorceries ... (v. iii. 27–9)

– his real enemy Vasques appears to invite him to the feast. The swift juxtaposition of hollow threats and the visual embodiment of his danger undercut any credibility. As the peevish schoolboy he can only utter defiance, '... tell them I dare come'. Vasques scarcely conceals his amusement at the immaturity of his victim. 'Dare come?', he echoes (v. iii. 47–8).

Comedy and realism prove the most important factors

throughout the opening acts, illustrating the superficiality of Giovanni's high-flown imagination. The intellectualizing of love is shown to be farcical through the eyes of Bergetto. Annabella, who of course is attractive but whom Giovanni indulgently praises as:

> That beauty which, if framed anew, the gods
> Would make a god of if they had it there,
> And kneel to it, as I do kneel to them. (I. i. 21–3)

– is seen by the clown as of little more attraction than a Parmesan cheese as Poggio reports:

> Forsooth, my master said that he loved her almost as well as he loved parmasent, and swore ... that she wanted but such a nose as his was, to be as pretty a young woman as any was in Parma. (I. iii. 60–3)

Later (II. iv. 27) it is not merely the nose but also the teeth which are deemed to need improvement. For the fool Neo-Platonic arguments are an aberration of natural inclinations. The clown sees love in physical terms, 'Yours upwards and downwards as you may choose' (II. iv. 29) and it is this earthy perspective that helps clarify Giovanni's situation. His pretentious sentiments:

> I have too long suppressed the hidden flames
> That almost have consumed me; I have spent
> Many a silent night in sighs and groans,
> Ran over all my thoughts, despised my fate,
> Reasoned against the reasons of my love,
> Done all that smooth-cheeked virtue could advise,
> But found all bootless ... (I. ii. 222–8)

– mean little more than Bergetto's words:

> ... by my troth I cannot choose but kiss thee once more for that word 'sweetheart'. *[Kisses her]* Poggio, I have a monstrous swelling about my stomach, whatsoever the matter be. (III. v. 43–6)

Similarly after all the vows and ritual and the enjoyment of the incestuous bed Putana focuses upon the physicality of the lovers' union as the important matter:

> Nay, what a paradise of joy have you passed under! Why, now I commend thee, charge; fear nothing sweetheart; what though he be your brother? Your brother's a man, I hope, and I say still, if a young wench feel the fit upon her, let her take anybody, father or brother, all is one. (II. i. 45–9)

Pertinently enough Annabella does not reprove the servant but rather thinks of the act in terms of reputation:

> *Annabella*   I would not have it known for all the world.
> *Putana*   Nor I indeed, for the speech of the people; else 'twere nothing. (II. i. 50–1)

Thus we discover the bourgeois aberrations of the brother and sister. There is no rebellion against the society for the sins are contained within its parameters. We find merely justifications being made to exonerate it in the context of the traditional beliefs which in a play such as *Dr Faustus* had been challenged at their roots. They are not heroes but symptoms of a false middle-class morality – a social code which as enacted by the other characters actually demands the rebellion which Giovanni and Annabella so confusedly circumscribed.

If love to Giovanni is expressed in the false platitudes of a distorted Platonism, it is exposed as repulsively male-dominated by the remainder of the characters. Soranzo's first appearance sees him altering pastoral concepts to suit personal satisfaction. Love must not have pain and thus Sannazaro's lines are rewritten from:

> 'Love's measure is extreme, the comfort pain,
> The life unrest, and the reward disdain.'

– to:

> 'Love's measure is the mean, sweet his annoys,
> His pleasure's life, and his reward all joys.' (II. ii. 1–2, 10–11)

The conceit is further exposed by Hippolita's immediate entry. Love in Parma has nothing to do with pastoral poetry, but is a matter of flesh and heat:

> Look, perjured man, on her
> Whom thou and thy distracted lust have wronged.
> Thy sensual rage of blood hath made my youth
> A scorn to me and angels; and shall I
> Be now a foil to thy unsated change? (II. ii. 27–31)

This is the male-orientated world described in Montaigne's essays where, as echoed by Marston in *The Dutch Courtesan*, men use women to satisfy lust, marry them for position and love them for chastity. If the woman transgresses she is discarded. Yet if the man does he is seen as expressing his natural inclinations although his female partner in the act is disgraced.[12] Following such a philosophy Soranzo sees no incongruity therefore in simultaneously rejecting Hippolita because of the wantonness he enjoyed and conjured within her, and wooing Annabella with words of loyalty, for her beauty and purity. The one was his whore, a dehumanized person, the other is to be his wife:

> I know I have loved you long, and loved you truly;
> Not hope of what you have, but what you are
> Have drawn me on: then let me not in vain
> Still feel the rigour of your chaste disdain.
> I'm sick, and sick to th' heart. (III. ii. 31–5)

Such attitudes in a male-orientated world are as perverse in their theatricality as are Giovanni's attempts to gain his sister's bed with a moral conscience. Annabella undercuts Soranzo with humour:

Annabella   Help, aqua-vitae!
Soranzo   What mean you?
Annabella   Why, I thought you had been sick!
Soranzo   Do you mock my love? (III. ii. 35–7)

Hippolita however is thrust away for Soranzo to receive his desire. When later he discovers that to be a bad bargain his reaction proves predictable:

> ... harlot, rare, notable harlot,

> That with thy brazen face maintain'st thy sin,
> Was there no man in Parma to be bawd
> To your loose cunning whoredom else but I?
> Must your hot itch and plurisy of lust,
> The heyday of your luxury, be fed
> Up to a surfeit, and could none but I
> Be picked out to be a cloak to your close tricks,
> Your belly-sports? (IV. iii. 4–12)

Morally the actual sin is not considered. The crime is that she has made him the recipient of a disgrace. It is his pride that is affronted. Appearance is the only moral criterion and it is the one to which Vasques appeals so as to rectify the harm in a manner justifying the pride and integrity of the master. To kill in passion would be demeaning to social status:

> Now the gods forfend!
> And would you be her executioner, and kill her in your rage too? O, 'twere most unmanlike! (IV. iii. 78–80)

Ford's moral irony however is seen in the manner in which Soranzo and Vasques plan to be revenged on Giovanni and Annabella at the birthday feast. A revenge which directly parallels that conceived by Hippolita and Vasques at the marriage. In the earlier case of the wronged woman the scene allows no justification in the ethics of male preservation. She is killed in the reversal of the plan and all applaud:

> *Vasques* ... end thy days in peace, vile woman;
>   as for life there's no hope, think not on't.
> *Omnes* Wonderful justice!
> *Richardetto*   Heaven, thou art righteous....
>
> *Florio* Was e'er so vile a creature?
> *Richardetto*   Here's the end
>   Of lust and pride. (IV. i. 86–8, 101–2)

The pride and lust have been as greatly if not more prominent in the male world as in the female yet all praise the deed as one of justice. True justice however does appear at Soranzo's later birthday feast where as his plans go astray, he himself meets his death.

Soranzo's attitude is indicative of the male-dominated morality that rules Parma. A pretence of feminine freedom is granted when for example Florio declares he wishes his daughter to marry not for 'wealth, but love' (I. iii. 11) but beneath such gestures is the constant bourgeois wisdom of strict paternity. Soranzo is the man she should marry:

> here she is,
> She knows my mind, speak for yourself to her,
> And hear you, daughter, see you use him nobly. (III. ii. 5–7)

It only takes her illness to give Florio the opportunity to enforce his will:

> *Florio* She shall be married, ere she know the time.
> *Richardetto* Yet let not haste, sir, make unworthy choice,
>   That were dishonour.
> *Florio*   Master doctor, no,
>   I will not do so neither; in plain words,
>   My lord Soranzo is the man I mean.
> *Richardetto* A noble and virtuous gentleman.
> *Florio* As any is in Parma. (III. iv. 11–17)

Doctor and father decide that physically she is ready to conceive and therefore will be married according to the father's choice. Authority in Parma's society is hierarchical and all have to obey so as to retain good order. This is so even though its leader, the Cardinal, lacks judicial integrity as his treatment of Grimaldi demonstrates.[13] Its moral adviser moreover, the Friar, shows himself divorced from the enquiries of the renaissance humanists. Giovanni's arguments at the beginning of the play consequently only obtain the traditional responses of conservatism:

> Such questions, youth, are fond; for better 'tis
> To bless the sun, than reason why it shines;
> Yet he thou talk'st of is above the sun –
> No more! I may not hear it. (I. i. 9–12)

It is sinful to enquire beyond the parameters of the established medieval faith which the great renaissance reformers, scientific or religious, had dared to do. The Friar thinks only in terms of an outdated iconography that ignores the Mephostophilean torments of the mind, in favour of red hot coals and burning pincers:

> There is a place —
> List, daughter! — in a black and hollow vault,
> Where day is never seen; there shines no sun,
> But flaming horror of consuming fires;
> A lightless sulphur, choked with smoky fogs
> Of an infected darkness: in this place
> Dwell many thousand thousand sundry sorts
> Of never-dying deaths: there damnèd souls
> Roar without pity, there are gluttons fed
> With toads and adders; there is burning oil
> Poured down the drunkard's throat, the usurer
> Is forced to sup whole draughts of molten gold;
> There is the murderer forever stabbed,
> Yet can he never die; there lies the wanton
> On racks of burning steel, while in his soul
> He feels the torment of his raging lust. (III. vi. 8–23)

These are the well expressed but medieval terrors[14] that affright the mind of Annabella but nowhere do we find their allegorical reality depicted with the psychological torment that wracked Faustus. Ford's aim seems to be not merely to expose the tragic folly of his protagonists but to demonstrate the confusion of their situation as part of a society which itself was morally distracted. Even less seems to be achieved by Giovanni than by Faustus or De Flores. Soranzo and Florio die but the Cardinal remains as a proof that the society and its structure has been relatively unaffected. Giovanni's conduct has proved to be a minor abrasion which in its healing, through the multiple deaths, can be put to use by the establishment:

> Take up these slaughtered bodies, see them buried;
> And all the gold and jewels, or whatsoever,
> Confiscate by the canons of the Church,
> We seize upon to the Pope's proper use. (v. vii. 147–50)

In the theatre these lines often produce laughter but their

validity to the play's incestuous vision remains.

The objection to the BBC production must be that however good the drama as a television entertainment it changed the tenor of the play. It allowed a repulsive society to triumph, even more than in Ford's original script, over the incestuous relationship. It transformed the lovers into totally sympathetic characters rather than allowing them to be understood in the context of their peers. Consequently moral parameters were drawn. Florio for example was informed by the doctor not that Annabella was suffering from 'a fullness of her blood' (III. iv. 8) but from a 'fullness of the belly'. He was consequently implicated in the trick played upon Soranzo. Hippolita was not allowed to die at the wedding feast thus helping to expose male double standards, but was rather disposed of in a bedroom closet away from the festivities. Soranzo did not die at the end of the play but triumphed arranging with the Justice a complete cover up for the events that had occurred. Grimaldi did not appear and Bergetto successfully eloped with Philotis, his sensuality rewarded, as was his servant, Poggio, bribed by the doctor to secure the match. The nineteenth-century manor house setting and the general alterations made some sense in depicting a secretive, hypocritical society protecting its own interests, but failed to convey the sterile nausea that is Ford's play.

On stage there have been four significant productions over the past twenty years.[15] In 1961 David Thompson produced a Bernard Miles adaptation of the play at the Mermaid on a dual level set designed by John Carruthers. In Elizabethan costume the actors used the full expanse of the large apron stage allowing for both a stylization and a rapidity of action, which appeared to occur like clockwork.[16] The distancing of the action forced an intellectual evaluation by the audience. The changing moment of the play in pace and tenor came with Hippolita's (Barbara Barnett) death. *The Times* correspondent (30 August 1961) noted that a tragic dimension was not achieved however, which we might now argue was to the good. John Woodvine gave a chilling performance as Vasques in total command of the action, coldly turning Putana's (Patience Collier) revelations against herself. Edward de Souza played Giovanni, David Sumner, Soranzo and Zena Walker in a low cut dress, a flirtatious, knowing, Annabella.

In 1972 Roland Joffé directed a mobile production for the

National Theatre (Old Vic) with Anna Carteret as Annabella; Nicholas Clay, Giovanni; Gawn Grainger, Vasques and Diana Rigg, Hippolita. Although full Elizabethan costume was employed the set depended on white drapes and transverse curtains which were manipulated to unfold 'the full width of the stage, providing half a dozen entrances' or to refold 'in depth to suggest antechambers and corridors'. Irving Wardle, (*The Times*, 19 July 1972) noted that this allowed simultaneously for 'Ford's austerity and the pace of his intrigue. The lovers were extremely young and the interpretation stressed the corruption of a society concerned only with money, authority and status, offset, as Wardle recorded, by an intense realization of the couple's relationship. The best performances came from Gawn Grainger, 'gnawing private grievance behind his hulking servile exterior' and James Hayes as a eunuch, Putana.

The Actors Company presented the work at the Edinburgh Festival in 1972 and later on tour, in a production by David Giles, set in an Edwardian world. Ian McKellen's Giovanni made his first appearance in bicycle clips as an intense young scholar who as the play progressed became increasingly and nervously more narcissistic and bestially sensual. Paola Dionisotti's Annabella sensitively displayed an almost matching vitality and potential desire for sexual release but only just bordering on her brother's obsessiveness. The set by Kenneth Mellor was of Parmesan collonades whilst black suits, white carnations and oiled hair gave an impression of a hypocritically slick society permitting dinner parties and evenings round the piano whilst ill deeds were accomplished behind the scenes. John Bennett's Vasques was the dutiful servant meticulously brushing his master's coat as he instructed him in the tactful art of revenge. Edward Petherbridge as Soranzo displayed the calm exterior of public respectability that highlighted the horrors of his private identity as he dragged Annabella across the floor by her hair on the discovery of her pregnancy. There was no cold distancing by costume as in 1961 but rather an attempt to convey the hot claustrophobia of a Godfather society where sunlight disguises inherent evil. Incest was one such sin shown in this production not to be anachronistic to the twentieth century.

The RSC's studio production was first seen at The Other Place in Stratford, in 1977.[17] It was directed by Ron Daniels with Simon Rouse as a pasty acned Giovanni and Barbara Kellerman as a dark eyed Annabella. A Mafia atmosphere was again prevalent within a mid-twenties Italian setting. The audience was on three sides, the fourth being fronted by railings behind which was a crucifix and a large statue of the Virgin Mary. Candles were lit and solemn church music played allowing for the confessional setting of the first scene. The ecclesiastical music was cleverly employed in juxtaposition with fairground organ tunes used as a theme for the sexual encounters and for the comic routines of Bergetto and Poggio. A wrought iron spiral staircase was a permanent fixture allowing for easy access to the balcony above the railings. It was from here that the languid Annabella was able to view the melancholy brooding Giovanni as he crossed the stage (I. ii.) head bowed in sulky meditation. When he made his proposition to her she laughed nervously but then allowed the tone to change comfortably into the seriousness of their ritualistic betrothal. The anaemic Giovanni absurdly unlike the 'celestial creature' that Ford ironically allows Annabella to describe was possessed throughout by a simultaneous discomfort with his desire and its fulfilment. In an innocent white dress Annabella was always hesitant, unsure, willing and yet reluctant, her wide eyes attempting to understand the complexity of her brother's thought. Characterized in such a way neither were greatly sympathetic which was to the credit of the production. Her death was achieved through the perversion of their sexual act – thighs interlocked Giovanni thrust his knife into her womb shabbily, peevishly and broodily killing her with a kiss. Appearing bloodied at the feast he was an inert pathetic figure ready to be hacked down by Geoffrey Hutchings's resourceful Vasques. Throughout Mr Hutchings played the servant as stocky, close-cropped, neat hatchet man totally loyal to his master in the social class above him. The portrayal neatly complemented Nigel Terry's greasy Soranzo with his dark suit, spats and button hole. Together they were the rulers of a repugnantly amoral society symbolized by Vasques's flick knife and his meditative hypocritical look to a religious icon as he heard Putana's (Valerie Lush) homely revelations of the incest. She was swiftly turned away to have her eyes put out. Tim Wylton's Bergetto[18] was simultaneously a pathetic relief from and poignant reminder of the vacuity of the society about him. A fat perspiring man, shirt tail hanging, he was rewarded with absolute loyalty from Ron Cook's beautifully conceived Poggio.

This funny little servant constantly thumbing his braces and running after his master allowed the audience to find some sympathy with him as in his disbelief he mourned his master's death. Thus the accidental killing brought a poignancy for the audience that allowed in contrast a realization of the debility that pervades the major part of the action. Although some of the comedy was in the realm of farce it allowed the play's themes to be brought into sharper focus and justified the line of interpretation. A number of critics did not like the production but it was one in the close confines of the studio that portrayed the sordid reality not only of the lovers' deeds, naked in the darkness of Annabella's chamber – Putana hurriedly making the bed before the entrance of Florio – but also of the carnation society dominated by the pompous scarlet of the Cardinal. Ron Daniels like David Giles before him, had realized the devitalizing effect of Ford's Parma and presented this late-renaissance drama with a comprehensible immediacy for a modern audience.

8 Postscript

During the course of this book, in an attempt to demonstrate the modernity of these seven seminal plays, reference has sometimes been made to twentieth-century concepts of absurdity. Aberrations of such ideas are found, as Andrè Gide tells us, within the writings of all 'great specialists of the human heart'.[1] The difference however between the renaissance authors and the modern dramatists of absurdity is one of faith. Not faith particularly in a divine Godhead, although their sense of morality is dominated by the Christian tradition, but in the order of time. In anthropological terms the absurdity of man's actions at periods of feast and festivity has been shown by E.R. Leach to have a linear pattern.[2] Man requires staging posts in time whereby he throws off respectability, his order, and embraces chaos so as to understand the nature of everyday life. At such feasts he wears funny hats, costumes, false noses and indulges in an experience of fantastic absurdity before re-establishing the normality of his existence. In many of Shakespeare's plays as C.L. Barber has demonstrated,[3] such a pattern of absurdity forms the kernel of the drama. From the sentence of Egeon to death and the account of his history we witness a farcical reversal of norms where man's existence itself is brought into question. Sanity becomes madness, madness sanity as the Antipholuses and Dromios strive to find a touchstone of proof, a solution to madness. In the reversed world of festivity enjoyment can be found and sorrow experienced. Such moments in time, therefore, do not necessarily have to be festive in a comic sense. They exist too in tragedy and tragicomedy. Isabella deluded by the role-play of the Duke wails the loss of her brother whilst Angelo triumphs in the sensual mechanism of his power. These worlds acted out in a brief period of time have the validity of real life but the play always brings the errors or falsehoods to an end, Egeon is recognised, the Duke discovered, Volpone sentenced,

Vindice, De Flores, Giovanni exposed and Faustus taken down to hell. The moment of recognition that brings the play to a close implies faith in the midst of doubt, order in the midst of chaos. The dramatists may wish the audience to see through the protagonists' respective fates a criticism of the society to which they belonged and they may question the rational fabric of existence itself, but they do not dismiss its foundations as inescapably futile. It is here that the resemblances between absurd drama and the renaissance fade. The notable absentee from many modern plays is the recognition scene. For Sartre, Ionesco, Genet and Beckett there is no moment of discovery signalling the end of a festival pattern and the consequent return to normality since there is nothing to be discovered. Thus Ionesco in *The Bald Prima Donna* ridicules the concept of *anagnorisis* as an absurd mechanical device indicative of man's inability to find order out of chaos, rather than as an agent to regain sanity. Mr and Mrs Martin in this play prove themselves to be man and wife through a satirical episode of discovery:

> *Mrs Martin* But what an amazing coincidence! I too have a little daughter and she is two years old and she has one red eye and one white eye; and she is very pretty and her name is Alice too, Sir!
> *Mr Martin* How very extraordinary and what a strange coincidence! And amazing! Could it be that she is one and same, dear Madam?
> *Mrs Martin* How very extraordinary! But it's quite, quite possible, Sir!
> *Mr Martin* Then, dear lady, I think there can be no mistake. We must have seen each other before and you are my very own little wife... Elizabeth, I've found you again!
> *Mrs Martin* Donald darling, it's really you![4]

For Ionesco *anagnorisis* holds neither theatrical nor thematic value. Discovery is a false premise. Thus even what you mechanically believe to be order is in fact chaos. After the grotesque ridicule of the Martins' recognition of each other he consequently allows the maid to tell the audience:

> Elizabeth is not Elizabeth and Donald is not Donald. And I'll prove it to you. The child Donald talked of

is not Elizabeth's daughter, not the same child at all.
Donald's little girl has one red eye and one white eye
just like Elizabeth's little girl. But whereas it's
the right eye of Donald's child that's red and the left
eye that's white, it's the left eye of Elizabeth's child
that's red and the right eye that's white. (pp. 96)

For Ionesco recognition, order, time itself are part of the grand illusion of life. His clocks whizz round and chime in halves, his characters rush about, collect possessions, philosophize and get nowhere. The striving to make sense of existence is as futile as Garcia's attempt to find something in hell in which to believe, or as Beckett's Vladimir and Estragon determining to wait on for Godot's arrival.

The renaissance dramatists as we have seen sometimes express such visions of sterility and often come close to despair but their inclinations towards total absurdity are always subservient to their faith that order, relying on time, will make sense of living or at least point towards a positivism within its progress. Midnight will come and what matters is how we spend our time in finding and employing our identities until its arrival. That the modern audience can still enjoy these renaissance plays and appreciate them testifies not only that the renaissance dramatists might have shared our sense of absurdity and pessimism but that we have not forgotten their sense of faith and optimism.

Abbreviations

ELR English Literary Renaissance

ES English Studies

E&S Essays and Studies

EinC Essays in Criticism

JEGP Journal of English and Germanic Philology

ELH A Journal of English Literary History

MP Modern Philology

PQ Philological Quarterly

RSC Royal Shakespeare Company

RST Royal Shakespeare Theatre

Notes and References

INTRODUCTION

1. The term renaissance is used for the title of this book in its broadest sense to include plays in the Elizabethan, Jacobean and Caroline periods. It should be mentioned that some critics prefer to limit the term to the earlier Tudor period of drama and that others see the works of Ford, for example, in terms of the baroque rather than the renaissance.

CHAPTER 1: THE COMEDY OF ERRORS

1. Jessica M. Davis, *Farce* (London, 1978) has adequately assessed the aesthetic value of farce as an art form depending on the delicate balance achieved between aggression and festivity in the context of its structure, 'Farce is indeed mechanical and its mechanical manipulations of plot and character distinguish it clearly from other, more flexible comic forms. Like all comedy, farce is both aggressive and festive. At its heart is the eternal comic conflict between the forces of conventional authority and the forces of rebellion' (pp. 23–4).
2. Bertrand Evans, *Shakespeare's Comedies* (London, Oxford, New York, 1960) pp. 8–9
3. Leo Salingar, *Shakespeare and the Traditions of Comedy* (Cambridge, 1974) p. 61.
4. References to *The Comedy of Errors* are to R.A. Foakes's edition, The Arden Shakespeare (London, 1962).
5. A comic piece of music operating in this way is Dohnányi *Variations on a Nursery Song* where the robust opening exposition is soon clarified by the lone piano simply stating the theme, the nursery song, *Ah, vous dirai-je, maman*, which in turn is succeeded by the intricacies of the variations on the theme.
6. Arthur Adamov, *L'Aveu* quoted from Martin Esslin, *The Theatre of the Absurd*, Penguin edition (London, 1968) p. 89
7. Adamov, for example, identifies his separation as a loss of what was once seen as God, a rational explanation for existence. See Esslin, pp. 89 ff.
8. William Empson, *Some Versions of Pastoral* (London, 1935) p. 34.
9. It is tempting to suggest that the twins could be seen as two facets of a single personality. Harry Levin, Introduction, *The Comedy of Errors*. The Signet Classic Shakespeare (New York and London, 1965) p. xxx, disagrees,

'That way schizophrenia lies ... the actual predicament is that of two personalities forced into the same role, rather than of one personality playing two roles, since the resident twin has the contacts and continuities and the roving twin intercepts them, as it were'.
10 Nowhere better than in R.A. Foakes, Introduction, *The Comedy of Errors*, The Arden Shakespeare, pp. xxxix-li, where in particular he links the 'loss or change of identity' of the characters 'with a disruption of family, personal and social relationships'. See also Alexander Leggatt, *Shakespeare's Comedy of Love* (London, 1974) pp. 1–19. Professor Leggatt would disagree however with the conclusions of the present discussion in that he states, 'One curious feature of the ending is that, while the problems of marriage have been thoroughly aired, there is no explicit reconciliation between husband and wife' (p. 9).
11 Harold Pinter, *The Birthday Party*, 2nd edition (London, 1965) p. 9.
12 Levin, op. cit., p. xxxi.
13 R.A. Foakes, Introduction, p. xxxix-xi, proposes a correct critical attitude, 'Any developed account of *The Comedy of Errors* is likely to seem portentous in relation to the complexities of Shakespeare's mature drama, and extravagant in relation to the usual classification of the play as early farce. Clearly it is important to keep a critical balance; but it is also important to recognize that, from the beginning of his career, Shakespeare was an artist of unusual power, and that all his work deserves serious attention.'
14 See Levin, op. cit., Introduction, pp. xxx–xxxi.
15 See John Higgins, 'Trevor Nunn in Search of Fresh Pastures', *The Times* (29 September 1976).
16 Quotations are from the original prompt-copy text of the performance, housed in the Shakespeare Centre Library, Stratford-upon-Avon. They are reproduced by kind permission of Trevor Nunn. A full cast list for this and other RSC productions is found in M. Mullin (ed.) with K. M. Muriello, *Theatre at Stratford-upon-Avon. A Catalogue to Productions of the Shakespeare Memorial/Royal Shakespeare Theatre, 1879–1978*, 2 vols. (London, 1980).
17 Not all critics were happy with the interpretation. John Barber, *Daily Telegraph* (1 October 1979), though praising the professionalism of the cast complained that the result was simply not amusing.
18 The production was also televised.

CHAPTER 2: DR FAUSTUS

1 A particularly influential work is D.M. Bevington, *From 'Mankind to Marlowe: Growth of Structure in the Popular Drama of Tudor England* (Cambridge, Mass., 1962) but generally a majority of critics show an acute awareness of the medieval heritage. Valuable articles surveying the critical approaches to the play are Max Bluestone, *'Libido Speculandi*: Doctrine and Dramaturgy in Contemporary Interpretations of Marlowe's *Doctor Faustus*', in *Reinterpretations of Elizabethan Drama*, ed. N. Rabkin (Selected Papers from the English Institute, New York, 1969) and J.S. Post, *Recent Studies in Marlowe 1968–76*, *ELR*, VIII (1977) pp. 382–399.
2 Sc. v. 128–9. Scene and line references to *Dr Faustus* are from the edition by John D. Jump, The Revels Plays (London, 1968, Manchester, 1976).

3 Jean-Paul Sartre, 'In Camera', in *Two Plays by Jean-Paul Sartre*, trans. S. Gilbert (London, 1946) pp. 108–9.
4 M.C. Bradbrook, *English Dramatic Form in the Old Drama and the New*, 2nd ed. (London, 1970) p. 54. I am greatly indebted to this invaluable book, particularly in Professor Bradbrook's categorization of the theatres of icon and of dream.
5 Judith Weil, *Christopher Marlowe: Merlin's Prophet* (Cambridge, 1977) p. 61, interestingly notes, 'Belly language is what we hear when Faustus signs the deed of gift and quips, *"Consummatum est*; this bill is ended." He recalls, of course, Christ's dying words on the cross (John 19: 30). Ironically, the implicit pun on digestion also suggests that he has gorged himself on the wrong kind of wisdom. In an outrageously comic treatment of learned folly, Rabelais has Pantagruel remark to Panurge that "Consummatum est ... is what St Thomas Aquinas said when he had eaten the whole of his lamprey." In *Dr Faustus* such theological punning can provide a ghoulish premonition of the hero's fate.'
6 I am employing the word 'wit' in the sense that Dr Johnson found appropriate to the metaphysical poets. See his *Life of Cowley*.
7 Bradbrook, *English Dramatic Form*, p. 14.
8 J.R. Mulryne and Stephen Fender, 'Marlowe and the "Comic Distance", *Christopher Marlowe*, Mermaid Critical Commentary, ed. B. Morris (London, 1968) pp. 49–64, have interestingly focused arguments on *Tamburlaine* and *Edward II* to relate Marlowe to the theatre of the absurd.
9 Eugene Ionesco, 'Exit the King', in *Plays*, vol. v, trans. D. Watson (London, 1963) p. 36.
10 Robert Ornstein, 'The Comic Synthesis in *Doctor Faustus*', *ELH*, xii (1955) p. 170, reprinted in *Marlowe: Doctor Faustus: A Casebook*, ed. J.D. Jump (London, 1969) pp. 165–72. Among the many critics discussing the relationship of the sub-plot to the main plot is Harry Levin, who in *Christopher Marlowe: The Overreacher* (London, 1961) pp. 145-46, writes, '... Elizabethan tragedy delegates a conventional function to comedy, and *Doctor Faustus* need be no exception to that rule. ... while the comic underplot reduces the main plot of Marlowe's drama to absurdity, the overplot is luminously adumbrated – sketched, as it were, in lightning against a black sky. It is the adumbration of Faustus' downfall, glimpsed in the aboriginal tragedy of the fallen archangel. Victor Hugo's formulation for western art, the intermixture of grotesque and sublime, could not adduce a more pertinent example.' M.C. Bradbrook, 'Marlowe's *Dr Faustus* and the Eldritch Tradition', in *Essays on Shakespeare and Elizabethan Drama in Honour of Hardin Craig*, ed. R. Hosley (London, 1963) pp. 83–90, succinctly places Marlowe's comic-horrific mood within its contemporary context.
11 Certain parallels may be drawn with other Marlovian protagonists. Note for example Tamburlaine's final words:

> Farewell, my boys! My dearest friends, farewell!
> My body feels, my soul doth weep to see
> Your sweet desires depriv'd my company,
> For Tamburlaine, the scourge of God, must die. (*Tamburlaine the Great*, Part ii, v, iii. 245–8)

12 Peter Brook, *The Empty Space*, Pelican edition (London, 1972) p. 65. Brook's examples refer to Beckett's characters.
13 Jerzy Grotowski, *Dr Faustus: Textual Montage*, trans. Richard Schechner, *Tulane Drama Review*, 8 (1964) repr. in Jerzy Grotowski, *Towards a Poor Theatre* (London, 1975) pp. 71-2.
14 It should be noted, however, that the production received a considerable number of favourable notices including those of Irving Wardle, *The Times* (6 September 1974).
15 Nigel Alexander, *The Performance of Christopher Marlowe's 'Dr Faustus'*, British Academy Chatterton Lecture on an English Poet, 1971 (London, 1972) pp. 10-11.
16 Alexander, p. 11

CHAPTER 3: THE REVENGER'S TRAGEDY

1 G. Wilson Knight, *Shakespearian Production* (London, 1964) p. 42.
2 If it is Tourneur's. The authorship debate appears inexhaustible. For the sake of convenience the present chapter follows the convention of attributing the work to Tourneur.
3 See C. Stanislavsky, *An Actor Prepares*, trans. E. Reynolds Hapgood (London, 1937) pp. 271-80.
4 The play's debt to the medieval morality tradition was acknowledged in L.G. Salingar's influential essay 'The Revenger's Tragedy and the Morality Tradition', *Scrutiny*, VI (1937-8) pp. 402-24.
5 Madeleine Doran, *Endeavors of Art: A Study of Form in Elizabethan Drama* (Madison, Wis., 1954) p. 357.
6 R.A. Foakes, Introduction to *The Revenger's Tragedy*, The Revels Plays (London, 1966) p. xxxii. References to the play are to this edition. For discussions of the nature of the protagonist see also Robert Ornstein, *The Moral Vision of Jacobean Tragedy* (Madison, Wis., 1960, repr. Westport, Connecticut, 1975) pp. 105-27 and Peter B Murray, *A Study of Cyril Tourneur* (Philadelphia, 1964) pp. 173-228.
7 The dramatist's use of irony throughout the play has provided the impetus for much critical discussion. See in particular Samuel Schoenbaum, *Middleton's Tragedies: A Critical Study* (New York, 1955) pp. 18-22, and Peter Lisca, 'The Revenger's Tragedy: A Study in Irony' *PQ* XXXVIII (1959) pp. 242-51.
8 L.J. Ross, Introduction to *The Revenger's Tragedy*, Regents Renaissance Drama Series (London, 1967) p. xxviii, comments, 'Vindice turns his "lady" from chaste victim into a whore and murderess just as he has turned himself into a pander and murderer'.
9 Act III Sc. v. is rightly regarded as the work's focal point. I.S. Ekebald (Ewbank) 'An Approach to Tourneur's Imagery', *MLR*, LIV (1959) p. 498, instructively writes, 'In *The Revenger's Tragedy* the climax of the play is not at the end, but very near the middle of the play: in the skull-scene. Instead of being the logical solution to a ladder-like argument, it is the hub from which meanings radiate out over the whole play.'
10 Tourneur's use of the pun and related modes of expression has been discussed by a number of critics including Foakes and Lisca, above, and

Una Ellis Fermor, *The Jacobean Drama* (London, 1936) pp. 153-69. The relationship between Vindice and Piato has also received varying degrees of critical attention, in particular by Salingar, Foakes and Ornstein.
11. There is possibly a sound theatrical reason for this. The original actor may well have preferred to use his own voice rather than a disguised one for the majority of the play.
12. Alvin Kernan, *The Cankered Muse: Satire of the English Renaissance* (New Haven. Conn., 1959) p. 227, consequently argues that Vindice is simultaneously both satirist and revenger: 'But Vindice ... discovers a further reality, the skull. Perceiving that "lust is death" and that therefore the characters of the play who are no more than ambulant sexual appetites are in reality dead, his satiric business of cutting away pretense can be realized only by cutting away the bodies of his enemies and reducing them to the reality of the skeleton. In this way the actions of the blood-revenger and the satirist are perfectly fused, and the pessimism and cruel methods of the Elizabethan satirist are given their ultimate expression.'
13. These words conclude the most discussed passage in *The Revenger's Tragedy*, Vindice's *memento mori*, III. v. 72–98. R.A. Foakes, notes p. 71, 'Among the more important analyses are those by T.S. Eliot (1919, in *Selected Essays*, 1951, p. 20); M.C. Bradbrook, *Themes and Conventions of Elizabethan Tragedy* (1936), pp. 170–1; Theodore Spencer, *Death and Elizabethan Tragedy* (1936), pp. 238–40; L.G. Salingar, *Scrutiny*, VI (1938), pp. 419-20; F.R. Leavis, *Scrutiny*, XIII (1945), pp 120–2; and John Peter, *Complaint and Satire* (1956), pp. 262–4. I have not attempted to duplicate the rich commentary they provide on this passage.'
14. I.S. Ekebald (Ewbank), 'An Approach to Tourneur's Imagery' p. 497, comments, '... there is no doubt that the ultimate purpose of the passage is to hold up vice to be denounced. Placed safely by the first image – the *gluttonous* dinner – the passage is firmly held within the moral scheme of the play by the fact, accepted by author and audience alike, that this is Sin personified speaking.' This rather grotesque interest in the means of one's own conception is still employed by modern dramatists to illustrate the spiritual sterility of domestic environments. Compare Spurio's speech for example with that of Lenny in Pinter's *The Homecoming* (London, 1966) p. 36: 'I'll tell you what, Dad, since you're in the mood for a bit of a ... chat, I'll ask you a question. It's a question I've been meaning to ask you for some time. That night ... you know ... the night you got me ... that night with Mum, what was it like? Eh? When I was just a glint in your eye. What was it like? What was the background to it? I mean, I want to know the real facts about my background. I mean, for instance, is it a fact that you had me in mind all the time, or is it a fact that I was the last thing you had in mind?'
15. Robert Ornstein, *The Moral Vision of Jacobean Tragedy*, p. 108, notes, 'Tourneur cannot convince us that his tragic universe holds a mirror up to nature, but he skilfully creates an illusion of depth in his two-dimensional scene by suggesting that the Duke's court extends and merges imperceptibly with a larger world which, if brought into the foreground, would be no different from the group of sensualists which Tourneur examines in detail.'
16. As has often been noted, the imagery of the play, finding its impetus from wealth, disease, sexuality and death, establishes an anti-world of reversed

norms. Thus Salingar, p. 418, writes '... the business of buying and selling, the accumulation of wealth without social responsibility, which has hoisted sensuality to its evil eminence in his court, is accepted as normative and final; it becomes a process by which the values of Nature and the impulses which go to maintaining a civilized life are inevitably decomposed into their opposites.'
17 From Brian Shelton 'A Preface to "The Revenger's Tragedy"', unpublished notes which he circulated to his actors before starting rehearsals. Brian Shelton tells me that not all his preliminary ideas on the work proved possible in performance, rehearsals showed some to be inappropriate others more important. Nevertheless the notes were able to establish a basis from which he and his cast were able to work with the text. I am grateful to the director and also to the administrators of the Pitlochry Festival Theatre for providing me with information about the performance and the ideas behind it.
18 B. Shelton, 'A Preface to *The Revenger's Tragedy*.'
19 To some extent this element in the design was forced on the director, though it worked extremely well. The rake of the auditorium at the old Pitlochry theatre was such that not all the audience could see the floor of the stage – a complication in a revenge tragedy which ends with bodies strewn in death.
20 References are to the prompt copies and stage managers' scripts of the play housed in the Shakespeare Centre Library, Stratford-upon-Avon, and are reprinted by kind permission of Trevor Nunn and John Barton. The newly-written additions to the work vary between the scripts for 1966, 1967 and 1969. I have tended to follow the minor revisions of 1967 in preference to 1966. For a more detailed account of this production see Stanley Wells, *'The Revenger's Tragedy* Revived'. *The Elizabethan Theatre* VI. *Papers given at the International Conference on Elizabethan Theatre held at the University of Waterloo, Ontario, in July 1975*, ed. G.R. Hibbard (Toronto, 1978) pp. 105–33.
21 The impetus for this speech came from II. iii. 37–46, lines which were consequently cut in the subsequent scene.
22 The highly praised music throughout, was composed by Guy Woolfenden. It should be noted that this scene brought the RSC's first act to a dramatic close followed by the interval.
23 Gareth Lloyd Evans, *Stratford-upon-Avon Herald* (12 May 1967).
24 In 1969 the part of the Duchess was taken by Patience Collier.
25 Compare for example the notices of *The Times* (28 November 1969) and *Daily Telegraph* (28 November 1969). The present book went to press before the 1980 production of the play at the Liverpool Playhouse. A notable production in the United States occurred in 1970 at the Yale Repertory Theatre directed by Robert Brustein with Kenneth Haig as Vindice.

CHAPTER 4: VOLPONE

1 L.C. Knights, *Drama and Society in the Age of Jonson* (London, 1937).
2 J.J. Enck, *Jonson and the Comic Truth* (Madison, Wis., 1957). Professor Enck noted in particular the tenor of European literature between the two world wars. His views have been independently endorsed by a number of critics

including for example George Parfitt, *Ben Jonson: Public Poet and Private Man* (London, 1976) who writes, p. 141, 'In the various modes of Jonson's plays there is always this exploration of what is, finally, doubt about the possibility of human communication and uncertainty as to whether life has any meaning at anything above animal level. The greatness of his drama comes from Jonson's reluctance (he being basically a strong moralist) to admit the disturbing possibility that his doubts and uncertainties may be justified. It is a greatness which has its individuality, but which has affinities with such great moderns as Zola, Sartre and Beckett (as well as with the visions of lesser men such as Pinter and Stoppard) and which, I believe, can work powerfully on the modern stage.'
3. Alvin Kernan, Introduction, *Volpone, The Yale Ben Jonson* (New Haven and London, 1972) pp. 1–26. G.R. Hibbard, 'Ben Jonson and Human Nature' in *A Celebration of Ben Jonson*, ed. W. Blissett, J. Patrick and R.W. Van Fossen (Toronto and Buffalo, paperback edition, 1975) pp. 55–81. Further interesting discussions of role-play are found in J.W. Creaser, 'Volpone: The Mortifying of the Fox', *E in C*, xxv (1975) pp. 329–56 and S.J. Greenblatt, 'The False Ending in *Volpone*', *JEGP*, LXXV (1976) pp. 90–104. Enck also concentrates on the disguise motif.
4. Jonas A. Barish, 'The Double Plot in *Volpone*', *MP*, LI (1953) pp. 83–92, repr. in *Volpone: A Selection of Critical Essays*, ed. Jonas A. Barish (Casebook Series, London, 1972) pp. 100–17 and in *Jonson: A Collection of Critical Essays* (Twentieth Century Views, Englewood Cliffs, N.J., 1963) pp. 93–105. As with many critics of the play I am indebted to this influential essay. A different view of the nature of the double plot from that seen by Barish, is found in J.W. Creaser, 'A Vindication of Sir Politic-Would-Be', *ES*, LVII (1976) pp. 502–14.
5. In the short story, *Metamorphosis*.
6. References to *Volpone* are to J.W. Creaser's edition, The London and Medieval Series (London, 1978). I have chosen this text in preference to 'Herford and Simpson'. It is largely indebted to the major edition and more easily accessible for undergraduate classes. My final view of Sir Politic-Would-Be is at variance with that of J.W. Creaser both in 'A Vindication of Sir Politic-Would-Be' and in the introduction to his edition where he argues, 'Politic's catastrophe in the tortoise-shell is a further sign of Jonson's affection and subtlety of evaluation. Politic is humiliated by Peregrine, yet, as throughout, simple Simon is preferable to smart Alec, and the punishment becomes a human triumph for the victim' (p.56).
7. Jean Genet, *The Balcony*, trans. B Frechtman (London, 1966) pp. 19–20. The affinity of some of the renaissance dramatists with Genet has been noted in recent years. Commenting on Mosca's soliloquy, (III. i.) Ian Donaldson, 'Volpone: Quick and Dead', *E in C* XXI (1971) p. 125, writes, 'As in the work of a writer such as Jean Genet, we are almost persuaded that the world is indeed composed merely of pimps and sadists and sharpers, and that what we are accustomed to think of as the "normal" world is a somewhat abnormal and, indeed rather underground affair.' Donaldson, p. 126, also sees a similarity between the opening act of *The Balcony* and the opening speech of *Volpone*: both can 'generate' their 'own excitement'. The present writer in *John Marston's Plays* (London, 1978) pp. 26–34, has also illustrated resemblances between Genet's *The Balcony* and

Marston's *The Malcontent*, whilst Martin L. Wine, Introduction, *The Malcontent* (Regents Renaissance Drama Series, London, 1965) p. xxv, has noted similarities between the Marston play and Genet's *The Blacks*.
8 Detachment is an important element in Jonson's dramatic style. M.C. Bradbrook, *The Living Monument: Shakespeare and the Theatre of his Time* (Cambridge, 1976) p. 31, writes, 'Ben Jonson's ... critical scrutiny of society withdrew the audience from the "game" of comedy, imposing on them a measure of detachment. It may be that a measure of detachment also enabled him to fill out his crowded canvasses with such a full picture of society. His comic world was meant to be looked at and not lived in; in the subhuman zoo of *Volpone*, the animals may be observed as if they were caged.'
9 Jean Genet, *The Maids*, trans. B. Frechtman (London, 1963) p. 42.
10 Martin Esslin, *The Theatre of the Absurd* (London, 1968) instructively gives the subtitle 'A hall of mirrors' to his chapter on Jean Genet.
11 The concept of Volpone as prostitute is expressed both by Enck and Hibbard.
12 *Drama and Society in the Age of Jonson*, p. 203. George Parfitt, *Ben Jonson: Public Poet and Private Man*, p. 59, comments, 'The avocatori are not the play's only representatives of the law. The law's function is to ascertain truth and to express society's disapprobation of immoral (here 'antisocial') behaviour. In this sense the law is society's public conscience, voicing what society wishes to be told is acceptable conduct within it. And in *Volpone* the law is indeed a mirror of society as Jonson presents it – corrupt, greedy, morally confused, vicious. There is scarcely a reference to the law in the play which does not prepare us to find that the avocatori will be ironically fitting judges for Volpone, Mosca and their dupes. Voltore, himself a lawyer, is a constant reminder that the law is not necessarily society at its best ... The avocatori ... seem spectators watching a drama rather than investigators of illegal activities and the truth reveals itself with almost no help from them. Their view of how law should work is affected by hierarchical considerations ...'
13 Harry Levin, 'Jonson's Metempsychosis', *PQ*, XXII (1943) pp. 231–9, repr. in *Volpone: A Selection of Critical Essays* ed. Barish, pp. 88–99, discusses both the serious and satirical interest in Pythagorian metempsychosis in Elizabethan and Jacobean writers. For a discussion of this episode see in particular J.W. Creaser, Introduction, pp. 44–5, E.B. Partridge, *The Broken Compass* (New York, 1958) pp. 78–80, and Clifford Leech, 'The Incredibility of Jonsonian Comedy' in *A Celebration of Ben Jonson* ed. W. Blissett *et al*, pp. 3–25, 'It is a piece of bitter and fantastical nonsense, having a truth nevertheless of its own. At least, that is how a Jacobean or a twentieth-century man must look back on the ancients: the philosopher's soul has descended into the body of the man-woman fool.' (p. 22)
14 J.W. Creaser, *Volpone: The Mortifying of the Fox*, p. 350, comments, 'But surely it is just vindictive that Volpone must literally become the part that he has played ... Justice in Jonson's day was often savage, but even so this court's concept of justice is exceptional ... The law becomes a butcher, treating criminals as cattle to be fattened before slaughter as 'food' for the populace'.
15 J.J. Enck, *Jonson and the Comic Truth*, pp. 124–5, comments, 'There is ... no

Notes and References

accountable force to deliver moralizing speeches and to round off all corners nicely. Viewed in this way, the rationale of the play must be accepted as largely negative; judgments have to be brought from outside the dramatic frame by the audience roused through what the stage denies them.' Earlier he notes, p. 121, 'There can be no correction because no standard exists in the city. Any explicit disapproval of Venetian lasciviousness must be read into *Volpone* from the implicit condemnation in every line of the verse.'

16 The pun on the word 'mortifying' is discussed in detail by J.W. Creaser, *Volpone: The Mortifying of the Fox*, p. 352.
17 See for example Leech, *The Incredibility of Jonsonian Comedy*, p. 19 and Creaser, *Volpone: The Mortifying of the Fox*, p. 353.
18 In this respect Donald Wolfit, one of the great Volpones in theatrical history was able to make a *coup de théâtre* as is recorded by R.B. Parker, 'Volpone in Performance: 1921–72', *Renaissance Drama*, NS, IX (1978) p. 170, '[Wolfit] managed to pull the tones together by his handling of the epilogue. He spoke it in his own person: not in character as Volpone, but as a variant of his own familiar hanging-from-the curtain call. With his face relaxed, the make-up could be seen as make-up; the actor was visible through the role; and, as he gracefully begged the audience's applause in his Volpone "poetry" voice, the defeat of the fox was absorbed into the success of the actor, and the link between Volpone-as-performer and Wolfit-as-performer was finally consolidated.' In his full and invaluable article R.B. Parker has discussed the major productions of the play in Canada, the USA and the UK since 1927.
19 See in particular Creaser, *Volpone: The Mortifying of the Fox*, pp. 343–4, Donaldson, *Volpone: Quick and Dead*, p. 123 and Enck, p. 129 for interesting comments on Celia and Bonario. For a discussion of Castiza's role in *The Revenger's Tragedy* see Chapter 3 above.
20 Olivier could have provided the correct balance but to my knowledge never played the role. It is a pity too that Eric Porter did not revive the part after his performance in 1955 at the Bristol Old Vic, which was possibly unduly influenced by his knowledge of Wolfit's production. Among other actors who have played the role the portly, robust Leo McKern made a physically comic impact at the Oxford Playhouse in 1966. See Parker.
21 E.B. Partridge, *The Broken Compass*, p. 83. Colin Blakely played Volpone in Guthrie's 1968 production.
22 Irving Wardle, *The Theatres of George Devine*, (London, 1978) p. 149.
23 Parker, p. 152.
24 Parker, p. 172.
25 Michael Billington, *Guardian*, 27 April 1977.

CHAPTER 5: MEASURE FOR MEASURE

1 See for example Josephine Waters Bennet, *Measure for Measure as Royal Entertainment* (New York, 1966).
2 'Directing Problem Plays: John Barton talks to Gareth Lloyd Evans', *Shakespeare Survey*, 25 (Cambridge, 1972) p. 65.
3 G. Wilson Knight, *The Wheel of Fire* (London, 1930).
4 The various sides of the critical debate concerning the duke is well

illustrated in a recent book by Rosalind Miles, *The Problem of Measure for Measure* (London, 1976).

5 References to *Measure for Measure* are to J.W. Lever's edition, The Arden Shakespeare (London, 1967).

6 These were stressed most acutely by Gareth Lloyd Evans (*Stratford-upon-Avon Herald*, 7 July 1978). In 1979 John Barber (*Daily Telegraph* 8 November 1979) was still expressing doubts about the over 'playful' nature of the performance but critics in general were expressing their admiration at the excellence of the production. Kyle's *Measure for Measure* had achieved a greater stability as time had progressed and confidence grown.

7 A letter from Bond to the director entertaining this view was printed on the back of the theatre programme. Bond and Marowitz (see below) are not the only modern playwrights to show particular interest in this play. Howard Brenton adapted the work for a production at the Northcott Theatre, Exeter in 1973.

8 See Antonin Artaud, *The Theatre and its Double*, trans. Victor Corti (London, 1970) p. 68: '...instead of harking back to texts regarded as sacred and definitive, we must first break the theatre's subjugation to the text and rediscover the idea of a kind of unique language somewhere in between gesture and thought'.

9 F.R. Leavis, *The Common Pursuit* (London, 1952) p. 169.

10 See Michael Billington, *Guardian*, 1979, 'where Jonathan Pryce's Angelo was itchy with sexual frustration, David Suchet ... plays him as a legal precisian amazed at what he finds in himself. "Do I love her?" he asks after Isabella has left the room, weighing the crucial verb as if it has never darkened his lips before.'

11 The text of The Open Space production with an introduction by Charles Marowitz is found in *Plays and Players* June 1975. The text is also reprinted in C. Marowitz, *The Marowitz Shakespeare* (London, 1978) pp. 181–225. There is an article by Charles Marowitz concerning his view of the relationship between law and justice and its influence on his production in the *Guardian*, 28 May 1975.

12 *Shakespeare Survey*, 25, p. 65.

13 RSC continuity, which enables different productions to feed healthily off each other proved a theatrical highlight of the decade. Witness for example the way in which Buzz Goodbody's studio *Hamlet* in 1973 was to lead to such major studio productions as Trevor Nunn's *Macbeth* (1976/7), John Barton's *The Merchant of Venice* (1977) and Ron Daniels's *Pericles* (1979–80).

14 The Riverside Theatre is a converted TV studio.

15 The designer was Alison Chitty.

16 The descriptions are from *The Times* 2 April 1970, *Plays and Players* October 1974 and the *Financial Times* 25 August 1976 respectively.

17 Charles Marowitz, *Plays and Players* June 1975, suggested Richard Nixon as an appropriate man to play his Angelo.

CHAPTER 6: THE CHANGELING

1 Robert Jordan, 'Myth and Psychology in *The Changeling*', *Renaissance Drama*, III (1970) pp. 157–65, 'In the center of the play ... are two figures locked in

a relationship, figures simplified down to a few qualities apiece so that the relationship itself takes on a monumental simplicity – brutishness and love at the feet of beauty and revulsion... Middleton is here hovering on the verge of one of the more potent mythic confrontations, that of beauty and the beast, the princess and the frog.' (p. 159)

2 Jordan, p. 165.
3 References to *The Changeling* are to N.W. Bawcutt's edition, The Revels Plays (London, 1958). Criticism of the play is rich and varied finding one of its most recent incisive outlets in the essay by Leo Salingar, *'The Changeling* and the Drama of Domestic Life', *E&S*, XXXII pp. 80–96. Books and further essays of particular value include William Empson, *Some Versions of Pastoral* (London, 1935); M.C. Bradbrook, *Themes and Conventions of Elizabethan Tragedy* (London, 1935); Helen Gardner, 'Milton's Satan and the Theme of Damnation in Elizabethan Tragedy', *E&S*, I (1948) pp. 46–66; Samuel Schoenbaum, *Middleton's Tragedies*, (New York, 1955); G.R. Hibbard, 'The Tragedies of Thomas Middleton and the Decadence of Drama', *Renaissance and Modern Studies* I (1957) pp. 35–64; N.W. Bawcutt, Introduction: *The Changeling*, The Revels Plays (London, 1958); R.H. Barker, *Thomas Middleton* (New York, 1958); Robert Ornstein, *The Moral Vision of Jacobean Tragedy* (Madison, Wis., 1960); Christopher Ricks, 'The Moral and Poetic Structure of *The Changeling*,' *E in C*, x (1960) pp. 290–306; Irving Ribner, *Jacobean Tragedy: The Quest for Moral Order*, (London, 1962); Patricia Thomson, Introduction and Notes: *The Changeling*, The New Mermaids (London, 1964); Richard Levin, *The Multiple Plot in English Renaissance Drama*, (Chicago, Ill., 1971); Christopher Ricks, 'The Tragedies of Webster, Tourneur and Middleton: Symbols, Imagery and Conventions', *Sphere History of English Literature*, III, English Drama to 1710, ed. C. Ricks, (London, 1971); D. Farr, *Thomas Middleton and the Drama of Realism*, (Edinburgh, 1973); N. Brooke *Horrid Laughter in Jacobean Tragedy* (London, 1979).
4 As in the case of Iago of course it is this disregard and consequent general acceptance of honest fidelity which provides De Flores's greatest strength.
5 Leo Salingar, *'The Changeling* and the Drama of Domestic Life' p. 8, writes, 'What finally betrays Beatrice-Joanna is precisely the confidence in her birth and status that she has absorbed from the society around her. And *The Changeling* is not merely a character-portrait of a perverse young woman, but a study in what can fairly be called class-consciousness.' I am greatly indebted to this essay.
6 'I shall change my saint, I fear me, I find
    A giddy turning in me.' (I. I. 155–6).
7 Montaigne, 'Upon Some Verses of Virgil', *Essayes*, trans. John Florio (1603), 3 Vols., introd. L.C. Harmer (London, 1910), III, pp. 85–6, writes, 'Let us confesse the truth, there are few amongst us, that feare not more the shame they may have by their wives offences, then by their owne vices; or that cares not more (oh wondrous charity) for his wives, then his own conscience; or that had not rather be a theefe and church-robber, and have his wife a murderer and an heretike, then not more chaste then himselfe. Oh impious estimation of vices. Both wee and they are capable of a thousand more hurtfull and unnaturall corruptions, then is lust or lasciviousnesse. But we frame vices and waigh sinnes, not according to their

nature, but according to our interest; whereby they take so many different unequall formes. The severity of our lawes makes womens inclination to that vice, more violent and faulty, then it's condition beareth; and engageth it to worse proceedings then is their cause.'
8 For discussion of 'change', 'will' and 'judgment' see M.C. Bradbrook, *Themes and Conventions of Elizabethan Tragedy*.
9 For a discussion of the sexual pun in the play see Christopher Ricks, 'The Moral and Poetic Structure of *The Changeling*'. Ricks's examination is extended from sex to society by Leo Salingar, '*The Changeling* and the Drama of Domestic Life'.
10 See W. Empson, *Some Versions of Pastoral*, pp. 48–52 and M.C. Bradbrook, *Themes and Conventions of Elizabethan Tragedy*, pp. 213–39 for the first essays to establish the relationship of the two plots. G.R. Hibbard, 'The Tragedies of Thomas Middleton and the Decadence of the Drama', p. 63, is one of those who dissents from the idea, 'Badly written, stale, flat and unprofitable, untouched by wit or humour, this [the sub-plot] is plainly intended as a concession to the audience which is regarded as incapable of remaining seriously interested in serious matters for long'. Irving Ribner, *Jacobean Tragedy*, p. 129, proposes the view of the sub-plot as a moral corrective, 'The world of *The Changeling* is full of evil, but the sub-plot reveals also the possibility of good, and this is one reason that Isabella and her lovers are so essential to the total play', whilst N.W. Bawcutt, Introduction, p. lxvii, writes, 'Two sets of characters are portrayed, one group living in a world of normal human relationships, the other in a fantastic environment of madness which might be expected to have a damaging effect upon conduct. Yet the first group behaves with a real and terrible madness that leads to the death of four people, while in a world of apparent madness sanity always manages to assert itself, so that no real damage is done'.
11 Bradbrook, p. 219.
12 See for example Milton Shulman, *Evening Standard*, 17 October 1978; B.A. Young, *Financial Times*, 17 October 1978; Peter Jenkins, *Spectator*, 21 October 1978 and John Elsom, *Listener*, 26 October 1978.
13 See Robert Cushman, *Observer*, 22 October 1978.
14 The reviewers disagreed as to whether the attempt was a success. *The Sunday Times*, 5 March 1961 praised Richardson's ability to infuse 'the lecherous tones of the sub-plot into the main story' whilst *The Times*, 22 February 1961 complained that the drama was 'marred for us by a secondary plot infected by madmen'.
15 This view was voiced both by Sylvia Clayton, *Daily Telegraph*, 21 January 1974 and Raymond Williams, *Listener*, 31 January 1974. Extracts of the play have also been televised for the Open University with Ian Richardson as De Flores and Estelle Kohler as Beatrice-Joanna.
16 The relationship of *The Changeling* with *The Maid's Tragedy* is discussed by Ornstein, pp. 170–90. Beaumont and Fletcher's play received a welcome revival in an RSC production by Ron Daniels at The Other Place in 1980. For productions of *'Tis Pity She's a Whore* see Chapter 7.

CHAPTER 7: 'TIS PITY SHE'S A WHORE

1 M.C. Bradbrook, *Themes and Conventions of Elizabethan Tragedy*, understandably felt in 1935 that with Ford, and *'Tis Pity She's a Whore* in particular, the Elizabethan drama 'had worked itself out'. This view however is taken to an unacceptable extreme by David L. Frost, *The School of Shakespeare* (Cambridge, 1968) p. 160, who justifies the play only through the audience's ability to bring to mind Shakespeare's *Romeo and Juliet*.
2 T.S. Eliot, *Elizabethan Dramatists* (London, 1963) pp. 120–33, considers *The Broken Heart* and *Perkin Warbeck* as 'superior' plays. Clifford Leech, *John Ford and the Drama of his Time* (London, 1957) p. 11, is hesitant in his evaluation, 'It may be that this is Ford's best play ... But it is not Ford's most characteristic play.' Later p. 121, he adds, 'Yet though, *'Tis Pity* is perhaps his most striking achievement ... it is in the other tragedies and ... plays ... that we shall find the essence of his genius most apparent.' Cyrus Hoy, "'Ignorance in Knowledge': Marlowe's Faustus and Ford's Giovanni", *MP*, LVII(1960) p. 146, writes ' *'Tis Pity* is, notoriously, one of the most powerful of Elizabethan plays, but I doubt that even its warmest admirers would term it "grand". By so much as it fails of grandeur, it fails in the achievement of the highest tragedy ...' Robert Ornstein, *The Moral Vision of Jacobean Tragedy* (Madison Wis., 1960) p. 203, is the closest in agreement with Eliot, 'Only in *The Broken Heart* does one feel that he perfectly executed his artistic intention. In *'Tis Pity* his reach exceeded his grasp; his techniques were not refined enough for the moral and aesthetic complexity of his subject.'
3 Brian Morris, Introduction, *'Tis Pity She's a Whore*, The New Mermaids (London, 1968). The two other editions are those of N.W. Bawcutt, Regents Renaissance Drama Series (London, 1966) and Derek Roper, The Revels Plays (Manchester, 1975). References to *'Tis Pity She's a Whore* are to Derek Roper's edition.
4 Havelock Ellis, Introduction, *John Ford*, The Mermaid Series (London, 1888).
5 See in particular R.J. Kaufmann, 'Ford's Tragic Perspective', *Texas Studies in Literature and Language* I (Winter 1960) pp. 522–37, repr. in *Elizabethan Drama: Modern Essays in Criticism* ed. R.J. Kaufmann (London, Oxford, New York, 1961) pp. 356–72. Refer also to G.F. Sensabaugh, *The Tragic Muse of John Ford* (Stanford, Calif., 1944).
6 Among these are Robert Ornstein, *The Moral Vision of Jacobean Tragedy* (Madison, Wis., 1960); Irving Ribner, *Jacobean Tragedy, The Quest for Moral Order* (London, 1962); Mark Stavig, *John Ford and the Traditional Moral Order* (Madison, Milwaukee and London, 1968); Dorothy M. Farr, *John Ford and the Caroline Theatre* (London, 1979).
7 Parallels between Giovanni and Faustus are made by Cyrus Hoy. Miss Bradbrook draws some parallels with Middleton's *Women Beware Women* and refers also to *The Changeling* as does Nicholas Brooke, *Horrid Laughter in Jacobean Tragedy* (London, 1979). The question of sympathy towards the protagonists is debatable. Clifford Leech believes Giovanni to be in the tradition of conventional tragic protagonists displaying *hubris*, a man 'apart from his fellows, making his challenge, facing his end'. Mark Stavig in contrast sees Ford as satirically 'undercutting Giovanni's position', a view

rejected as too narrow by Derek Roper. Annabella is also problematic. T.S. Eliot regarded her as 'pliant, vacillating and negative ... virtually a moral defective', a view seen as 'too severe' by N.W. Bawcutt. But if with Mark Stavig we regard her as 'a noble victim' after her repentance we need to qualify our response in that she acquiesces to the wishes of a friar whose concept of religion, as Ribner demonstrates, 'involves a debasement of man, a denial of his intellectual capacity ...'.

8 H.J. Oliver, *The Problem of John Ford* (Melbourne, 1955) p. 89, provides a different interpretation of this lie, 'Giovanni characteristically reports to Annabella later that the Church "tells me I may love you"; the Friar's failure to prove a case against him is to Giovanni equivalent to condonation'.

9 Kaufmann, *Elizabethan Drama*, p. 367, writes that to each other Giovanni and Annabella, 'have significance only in relation to this arbitrary vow whereby they have separated themselves from any hope of unconventional felicity. This counterfeit marriage represents a radical misalliance which is made narrowly sacred by an arbitrary vow'.

10 See J.E. Cunningham, *Elizabethan and Early Stuart Drama* (London, 1965) p. 110. R Huebert, *John Ford, Baroque English Dramatist* (Montreal and London, 1977) p. 147, describes the symbol in Giovanni's terms: 'Annabella's heart is torn from her body in order to confirm Giovanni's belief in her purity, just as the entrails of the sacrificial lamb are torn and scattered to confirm the Hebrew belief in a pure Messiah. Annabella's perfect body has become the unblemished sacrifice. Yet, her flesh is torn not to atone for the evils of her society or to appease the wrath of an angry God, but simply to breathe the life of martyrdom into a private and chimerical mythology of love.'

11 N.W. Bawcutt, Introduction, Regents Renaissance Drama Series, p. xx, comments, 'Anything that stands in the way of his love is discarded or ignored: religion forbids an incestuous love, so he becomes an atheist, and when he is presented with Annabella's letter (in v. iii.), which strikes at the root of his moral position, he brushes it aside by arguing that it is forged. The temporary success of his love induces in him a kind of euphoria in which he believes that, far from being driven by fate, he is in fact the controller of fate ... This megalomania persists into the last scene of the play ... but there is a note of pathetic disillusionment when he realizes the truth.'

12 See in particular Montaigne's essay, 'Upon Some Verses of Virgil', *Essays*, trans. John Florio (1603), 3 Vols., introd. L.C. Harmer (London, 1910), III, pp. 62–128.

13 III. x. 30–70. Derek Roper Introduction, The Revels Plays, p. l, fn, is one of the few critics who do not consider society as an important issue in the play, 'What we see of society in *'Tis Pity* is imperfect, but I do not think this an important theme – as it is in Jonson's comedies, *The Revenger's Tragedy* or *The White Devil*'. For a different view see Irving Ribner, *Jacobean Tragedy* (1962), p. 164 ff., Kaufmann, pp. 366–9 and Morris, pp. xvi–xxii. Mark Stavig, p. 109, makes the point that an evil society does not excuse the protagonists's actions, 'The initial contrast of their nobility with the degradation around them does not lead to a defense of their immoral relationship as something purer and more ideal. Rather it reveals their weakness in betraying their earlier values and descending to the level of the society around them. Ford

skilfully depicts the deterioration of reason and virtues.'
14 Leech, pp. 57–8, in discussing this passage in relation to Ford's earlier poem, *Christes Bloodie Sweat* states, 'We cannot doubt that, when he wrote the play, the vision still had validity for him'. Other critics however do doubt, among them Ribner, p. 164, who sees Ford's characterization of the Friar as 'his means of showing religious inadequacy' and Ornstein, pp. 207–8, 'It requires a peculiar insensitivity to the nuances of characterization and verse in *'Tis Pity* to treat Giovanni as Ford's spokesman. But it is no less an error to turn Ford into a champion of orthodoxy by identifying him with the Friar, who is, despite his choric role, a somewhat muddled moralist.'
15 Donald Wolfitt's company presented the play in 1940, with Wolfitt as Giovanni; Rosalind Iden, Annabella; Michael Ashwin, Bergetto; H. Worrall-Thompson, Vasques and H. Langley, Soranzo. Since the war other productions include ones at Bristol Old Vic, 1968, directed by John David; Bradford Playhouse and Film Theatre, directed by John Howard, 1976; Theatre Gwynedd, Bangor, North Wales, 1979; and RADA, 1980. In July 1976 Alleyn's School, Dulwich appeared as Beeston's Boys in a Cockpits Arts Workshop production directed by Michael Lempriere and John Newton and presented on a stage reconstruction of the Cockpit designed by C. Walter Hodges. It was produced by BBC Radio in 1962 and 1970. Derek Roper, pp. lvii–lxii, provides a brief account of some of these productions and others in the USA and on the continent, including the film version by Giuseppe Patroni Griffi.
16 See Milton Shulman *Evening Standard*, 30 August 1961.
17 It was presented in Newcastle-upon-Tyne and in London during 1978.
18 Peter Clough took the part in 1978.

CHAPTER 8: POSTSCRIPT

1 André Gide, Introduction, *Montaigne: Essays*, trans. J. Florio (1603), selected and introduced by André Gide, Introduction trans. Dorothy Bussy, (New York, 1965) p. 10.
2 E.R. Leach, *Rethinking Anthropology*, London School of Economics Monographs on Social Anthropology, No. 22 (London, 1961) pp. 132–36.
3 C.L. Barber, *Shakespeare's Festive Comedy: A Study of Dramatic Form in its Relation to Social Custom* (Princeton, 1972).
4 Eugene Ionesco, *Plays*, trans. D. Watson, (London, 1958) Vol. i. p. 96.

Index

Absurd, Theatre of the, 4, 8, 23–5
  passim, 105–7
Actors Company, 102
Adamov, Arthur, 4, 8, 109n.
Alexander, Nigel, 28–9
Alienation, 35
Alleyn's School, 123n
Anagnorisis, 13, 106–7
Annis, Francesca, 69
Archer, Robin, 73
Aristotle, Arisotelean, 4, 13, 21
Artaud, A., 118n.
Ashwin, Michael, 123n.
Asquith, Conrad, 74
Aubrey, James, 29–30
Ayckbourn, Alan, 1

Baker, George, 64
Baker, Stanley, 88
Barber, C.L., 105
Barber, John, 47, 68, 110n., 118n.
Barge, Gillian, 70
Barish, Jonas, 48
Barnett, Barbara, 101
Barton, Anne, 61–2, 70
Barton, John, 26–27, 30, 42–6, 61–3, 68, 70–1, 74, 118n.
Bawcutt, N.W., 120n., 122n.
BBC, 63, 88, 89, 101, 123n.
Beaumont and Fletcher
  The Maid's Tragedy, 88
Beckett, S., 29, 106, 115n.
  Waiting for Godot, 107
Beeston's Boys, 123n.
Bennett, John, 102
Billington, Michael, 60, 64, 89, 118n.
Birmingham Repertory Company, 63
Björnsen, Maria, 72
Blakely, Colin, 117n.

Blatchley, Joseph, 87
Bond, Edward, 65, 118n.
Bosch, Hieronymous, 29
Bradbrook, M.C., 21, 23, 116n., 121n.
Bradley, David, 68
Brenton, Howard, 118n.
Brodrick, Susan, 73
Brook, Peter, 25, 72
Brooke, N., 121n.
Bruce, Brenda, 45
Brustein, R., 114n.
Bryden, Ronald, 46
Burge, Stuart, 63, 67, 73
Burke, David, 68, 88
Bury, John, 60

Carruthers, John, 101
Carteret, Anna, 102
Castle of Perseverance, The, 18
Chapman, Don, 46
Chekhov, Anton
  The Cherry Orchard, 73
Chitty, Alison, 118n.
Clay, Nicholas, 102
Clayton, Sylvia, 120n.
Clough, Peter, 123n.
Colley, Kenneth, 63
Collier, Patience, 101, 114n.
Commedia dell'arte, 16
Cook, Ron, 103
Cox, Brian, 86–7
Creaser, J.W., 115n., 116n.
Crutchley, Kate, 88
Culshaw, Bernard, 72
Cunningham, J.E., 122n.
Cushman, Robert, 57, 64, 120n.

Dali, Salvador, 29
Daniels, Ron, 102–4, 118n., 120n.

Index

David, Richard, 59–60
Davis, Carl, 73
Davis, Jessica, M., 109n.
Dench, Judi, 14
Deus ex Machina, 72
Devine, George, 59
Dionisotti, Paola, 67, 102
Dohnányi, 109n.
Don, Robin, 74
Donaldson, Ian, 115n.
Doran, Madeleine, 31
Drury, Patrick, 69
Duce, Sharon, 86

Edinburgh/Edinburgh Festival, 63, 68, 70, 73, 74, 88, 102
Ekebald, I.S. (Ewbank), 112n., 113n.
Eliot, T.S., 89, 121n.
Ellis, Havelock, 89
Elsom, John, 120n.
Empson, William, 4, 119n., 120n.
Enck, John, J., 47, 116n.
English Faust Book, 27
Esslin, Martin, 116n.
Evans, Bertrand, 1–2, 12
Evans, Gareth Lloyd, 46
Everyman, 23
Eyre, Richard, 88

Fettes, Christopher, 29–30
Foakes, R.A., 32, 110n., 113n.
Ford, John
   The Broken Heart, 121n.
   Christes Bloodie Sweat, 123n.
   Perkin Warbeck, 121n.
   'Tis Pity She's a Whore, 78, 88, 89–104, 106
Foxxe, David, 74
Frost, D.L., 121n.

Genet, Jean, 50–7 *passim*, 106, 115n.
   The Balcony, 50, 72, 115n.
   The Blacks, 50, 116n.
   Deathwatch, 50
   The Maids, 50–2, 53–5
Gide, André, 105
Giles, David, 102, 104
Gill, Peter, 64, 67, 69, 73–4, 74, 86–8
Goodbody, Buzz, 118n.
Goya, 88

Grainger, Gawn, 102
Griffi, G.P., 123n.
Grotowski, Jerzy, 26
Guthrie, Tyrone, 58, 60

Hack, Keith, 65, 69, 71, 74
Haig, K., 114n.
Hall, Peter, 47, 60
Hamilton, Robert, 74
Hands, Terry, 86, 87
Hardiman, Terence, 74
Harrison, Brian, 40
Hayes, James, 102
Hibbard, George, 47, 116n., 120n.
Higgins, John, 110n.
Hobson, Harold, 45, 68
Hodges, C. Walter, 123n.
Howard, Alan, 45
Hoy, C., 121n.
Huebert, R. 122n.
Hugo, Victor, 111n.
Hutchings, Geoffrey, 103

Iden, Rosalind, 123n.
Ingham, Barrie, 65
Ionesco, E.
   The Bald Prima Donna, 106–7
   Exit the King, 23–5
   Rhinoceros, 58

Jacobs, Sally, 72
James, Emrys, 27, 87
Jenkins, Peter, 120n.
Joffé, Roland, 101
Johnson, Dr, 111n.
Jonson, Ben
   The Devil is An Ass, 73
   Volpone, 47–60, 85, 105
Jordan, Robert, 76

Kafka, F., 48
   Metamorphosis, 58
Kaufmann, R.J., 122n.
Kellerman, Barbara, 102–3
Kelly, Dee, 41
Kember, Paul, 86
Kernan, Alvin, 47, 113n.
Knight, G. Wilson, 31, 62
Knights, L.C., 47, 53
Kohler, Estelle, 68, 70, 120n.

126 *Renaissance Drama and a Modern Audience*

Kyle, Barry, 67, 69, 71, 74

Langdon, Anthony, 74
Langley, H., 123n.
Leach, E.R., 105
Leavis, F.R., 68
Leech, Clifford, 116n., 121n., 123n.
Leggatt, Alexander, 110n.
Lempriere, Michael, 123n.
Levin, Harry, 8, 13, 109n., 111n., 116n.
Lindsay, Robert, 86
Lloyd, Bernard, 63
Lush, Valerie, 103

McCallin, Clement, 27
McEnery, John, 63
McKellen, Ian, 26, 102
McKern, Leo, 117n.
Magee, Patrick, 29
Marlowe, Christopher
  Dr Faustus, 18–30, 58, 90, 96, 100, 106
  Mephistophilean, 100
  Edward II, 32, 111n.
  Tamburlaine, 111n.
Marowitz, Charles, 65–7, 69–70, 74
Marshall, Anna Calder, 67, 68, 70, 88
Marston, John
  Antonio's Revenge, 12
  The Dutch Courtesan, 97
  The Malcontent, 116n.
Mason, Brewster, 87
Meaden, Dan, 74
Mellor, Kenneth, 102
Middleton, T.
  Women Beware Women, 121n.
Middleton, T., and Rowley, W.
  The Changeling, 76–88, 121n.
  De Flores, 90, 91, 100, 106
Miles, Bernard, 101
Miller, Jonathan, 67, 70, 71, 72, 74
Mirren, Helen, 45, 67, 69, 88
Montaigne, 97, 119n.
Morgan, Gareth, 27, 29, 30
Morley, Christopher, 71–2
Morris, Brian, 89

Nelligan, Kate, 63
Neo-Platonism, 90
  Neo-Platonic, 53, 95

Platonism, 96
Nettles, John, 74
Newcastle-upon-Tyne, 64, 123n.
Newton, John, 123n.
Nixon, Richard, 118n.
Noble, Adrian, 88
Nunn, Trevor, 14–6, 42–6, 118n.

O'Brien, Timothy, 71
Oliver, H.J., 122n.
Olivier, Lord, 117n.
Open University, 120n.
Ornstein, Robert, 113n., 123n.
Ovid, 23

Parfitt, George, 115n., 116n.
Parker, R.B., 60, 117n.
Partridge, E.B., 58
Pennington, Michael, 64
Petherbridge, Edward, 102
Pinter, Harold, 115n.
  The Birthday Party, 6–7
  The Homecoming, 113n.
Piper, Emma, 86
Plautus, Plautine, 1, 2
  Amphitruo, 9
  Brothers Menaechmi, 9
Porter, Eric, 28–9, 117n.
Pryce, Jonathan, 69, 118n.
Pythagorus, 53

RADA, 123n.
Ribner, Irving, 120n., 122n.
Richardson, Ian, 45, 68–69, 120n.
Richardson, Sir Ralph, 59
Richardson, Tony, 88
Ricks, Christopher, 120n.
Rigg, Diana, 102
Rodway, Norman, 45
Roper, D., 122n., 123n.
Ross, L.J., 112n.
Rouse, Simon, 102–3
Royal Shakespeare Company, 13, 14–7, 26–9, 30, 42–6, 61–75 *passim*, 86–7, 89, 102–4, 118n., 120n.
  Aldwych, Theatre, 64, 69, 86, 88
  The Other Place (RSC Studio Theatre), 102, 120n.
  Shakespeare Memorial Theatre, 59
  Theatre-go-round, 27

Index

Salingar, L.G., 2, 114n., 119n., 120n.
Sartre, J.-P., 106, 115n.
  In Camera, 19–20, 23, 107
Say, Rosemary, 87
Schöenberg, A., 73
Scofield, Paul, 47, 57
Selby, Nicholas, 45
Shakespeare, William, 12, 105
  Antony and Cleopatra, 5
  The Comedy of Errors, 1–17, 105
  Hamlet, 12
  Henry IV (Hal and Falstaff), 6
  King John, 38
  King Lear, 38
  Macbeth (Lady Macduff), 5
  Measure for Measure, 61–75, 86, 105
  A Midsummer Night's Dream, 72
  Othello (Iago), 52, 88
  Richard II, 9, 23
  Romeo and Juliet, 121n.
  Twelfth Night, 14
  The Winter's Tale, 12
Shaw, Robert, 88
Shaw, Sebastian, 62–3, 64
Shelton, Brian, 40–2, 114n.
Shorter, Eric, 73
Shulman, Milton, 64, 120n.
Souza, Edward de, 101
Spurling, Hilary, 46
Stanislavsky, C., 31–2
Stanton, Barry, 74
Stavig, Mark, 122n.
Stratford, Connecticut, *see* Theatres
Stratford-upon-Avon (RST), *see* Royal Shakespeare Company
Stoppard, Tom, 115n.
Suchet, David, 69, 74, 118n.
Sumner, David, 101

Theatres
  Aldwych, *see* Royal Shakespeare Company
  Bradford Playhouse and Film Theatre, 123n.
  Bristol Old Vic, 59, 88, 117., 123n.
  Cockpit Arts Workshop, 123n.
  Fortune, 29
  Liverpool Playhouse, 114n.
  Lyric Studio, Hammersmith, 29
  Mermaid, 101
  National Theatre, 47 (Old Vic), 102
  Northcott Theatre, Exeter, 118n.
  The Open Space, 65, 70, 74, 118n.
  The Other Place, *see* Royal Shakespeare Company
  Oxford Playhouse, 117n.
  Pitlochry Festival Theatre, 40, 46
  Riverside Studios, 64, 73, 86, 118n.
  Royal Court, 88
  Royal Lyceum, Edinburgh, 89
  Royal Shakespeare Theatre/ Shakespeare Memorial Theatre, *see* Royal Shakespeare Company
  Stratford, Connecticut, 13
  Theatre Gwynedd, 123n.
  Victoria Theatre, Stoke-on-Trent, 88
  Yale Repertory Theatre, 114n.
Terry, Nigel, 103
Thompson, David, 101
Tourneur, Cyril
  The Atheist's Tragedy, 45
  The Revenger's Tragedy, 31–46, 52, 85, 106, 122n.
Troughton, David, 86

Wagner, R., 29
Walker, Zena, 101
Waller, David, 45, 74
Wardle, Irving, 59, 68, 102, 112n.
Webster, John
  The White Devil, 122n.
Wells, Stanley, 114n.
Weil, Judith, 111n.
Weill, Kurt, 72–3
Wilde, Oscar, 21
Williams, Clifford, 16, 28–9, 30
Williams, Raymond, 120n.
Wine, Martin, 116n.
Woodvine, John, 101
Woolfenden, Guy, 114n.
Wolfitt, Donald, 117n., 123n.
Worrall-Thompson, H., 123n.
Wylton, T., 103

Young, B.A., 46, 69, 120n.

Zola, E., 115n.